THE
A B I D E
B I B L E J O U R N A L

GENESIS

Phil Collins, PhD
General Editor

TAYLOR UNIVERSITY CENTER FOR
**SCRIPTURE
ENGAGEMENT**

Bible**Gateway**

THOMAS NELSON
Since 1798
WWW.THOMASNELSON.COM

20 21 22 23 24 25 26 27 /AMC/ 15 14 13 12 11 10 9 8 7 6 5 4 3 2 1

HOW TO USE THIS JOURNAL

The NET Abide Bible Journals provide you with key tools for engaging Scripture. You'll find at the beginning of every Bible book an introduction that highlights the book's enduring message and themes as well as information about the author. Along with Scripture you'll also find prompts or sidebars designed to help you engage passages and deepen your understanding and experience of God's Word.

These prompts include the following:

 Contemplate. Following an ancient spiritual pattern (read, meditate, pray, contemplate), you'll ponder specific passages, take time to experience the Lord's presence, and pray according to what you discover.

 Journal. These sections draw attention to particular themes in the passages or questions the text raises. Each prompt is followed by blank lines on which you can record your thoughts as you focus, reflect on, and engage the Bible passage. Journaling encourages honesty, soul-searching, and openness to God's Word.

 Picture It. This section helps you place yourself within the biblical narrative or passage, imagining the sights, sounds, and smells of the Bible events. You will be no longer just a reader but also a witness, participant, or bystander in the story.

 Praying Scripture. All Scripture-engagement practices lead to speaking to and hearing from God. Conversation with God is essential for developing a deeper relationship with Him. These sidebars show you how to pattern your prayer after particular texts of Scripture.

We invite you to use the prompts provided and the journaling space as you see fit. This is a tool for you to use in deepening your relationship with God. Through the *Abide Bible* prompts, all of which are based on the time-tested methods, our hope is that you will genuinely engage with Scripture. As lives are transformed by God through His Word, we believe the church and the world will be influenced for our good and His glory.

TO THE READER

AN INTRODUCTION TO THE NEW ENGLISH TRANSLATION

"You have been born anew . . . through the
living and enduring word of God."

1 Peter 1:23

The New English Translation (NET) is the newest complete translation of the original biblical languages into English. In 1995 a multi-denominational team of more than twenty-five of the world's foremost biblical scholars gathered around the shared vision of creating an English Bible translation that could overcome old challenges and boldly open the door for new possibilities. The translators completed the first edition in 2001 and incorporated revisions based on scholarly and user feedback in 2003 and 2005. In 2019 a major update reached its final stages. The NET's unique translation process has yielded a beautiful, faithful English Bible for the worldwide church today.

What sets the NET Bible apart from other translations? We encourage you to read the full story of the NET's development and additional details about its translation philosophy at netbible.com/net-bible-preface. But we would like to draw your attention to a few features that commend the NET to all readers of the Word.

TRANSPARENT AND ACCOUNTABLE

Have you ever wished you could look over a Bible translator's shoulder as he or she worked?

Bible translation usually happens behind closed doors—few outside the translation committee see the complex decisions underlying the words that appear in their English Bibles. Fewer still have the opportunity to review and speak into the translators' decisions.

Throughout the NET's translation process, every working draft was made publicly available on the Internet. Bible scholars, ministers, and laypersons from around the world logged millions of review sessions. No other translation is so openly accountable to the worldwide church or has been so thoroughly vetted.

And yet, the ultimate accountability was to the biblical text itself. The NET Bible is neither crowdsourced nor a "translation by consensus." Rather, the NET translators filtered every question and suggestion through the very best insights from biblical linguistics, textual criticism, and their unswerving commitment to following the text wherever it leads. Thus, the NET remains supremely accurate and trustworthy, while also benefiting from extensive review by those who would be reading, studying, and teaching from its pages.

BEYOND THE "READABLE VS. ACCURATE" DIVIDE

The uniquely transparent and accountable translation process of the NET has been crystalized in the most extensive set of Bible translators' notes ever created. More than 60,000 notes highlight every major decision, outline alternative views, and explain difficult or nontraditional renderings. Freely available at netbible.org and in print in the *NET Bible, Full Notes Edition*, these notes help the NET overcome one of the biggest challenges facing any Bible translation: the tension between *accuracy* and *readability*.

If you have spent more than a few minutes researching English versions of the Bible, you have probably encountered a "translation spectrum" —a simple chart with the most wooden-but-precise translations on the far left (representing a "word-for-word" translation approach) and the loosest-but-easiest-to-read translations and paraphrases on the far right (representing a "thought-for-thought" philosophy of translation). Some translations intentionally lean toward one end of the spectrum or the other, embracing the strengths and weaknesses of their chosen approach. Most try to strike a balance between the extremes, weighing accuracy against readability—striving to reflect the grammar of the underlying biblical languages while still achieving acceptable English style.

But the NET moves beyond that old dichotomy. Because of the extensive translators' notes, the NET never has to compromise. Whenever faced with a difficult translation choice, the translators were free to put the strongest option in the main text while documenting the challenge, their thought process, and the solution in the notes.

The benefit to you, the reader? You can be sure that the NET is a translation you can trust—nothing has been lost in translation or obscured by a translator's dilemma. Instead, you are invited to see for yourself, and gain the kind of transparent access to the biblical languages previously only available to scholars.

MINISTRY FIRST

One more reason to love the NET: modern Bible translations are typically copyrighted, posing a challenge for ministries hoping to quote more than a few passages in their Bible study resources, curriculum, or other programming. But the NET is for everyone, with "ministry first" copyright innovations that encourage ministries to quote and share the life-changing message of Scripture as freely as possible. In fact, one of the major motivations behind the creation of the NET was the desire to ensure that ministries had unfettered access to a top-quality modern Bible translation, without needing to embark on a complicated process of securing permissions.

Visit netbible.com/net-bible-copyright to learn more.

TAKE UP AND READ

With its balanced, easy-to-understand English text and a transparent translation process that invites you to see for yourself the richness of the biblical languages, the NET is a Bible you can embrace as your own. Clear, readable, elegant, and accurate, the NET presents Scripture as meaningfully and powerfully today as when these words were first communicated to the people of God.

Our prayer is that the NET will be a fresh and exciting invitation to you—and Bible readers everywhere—to "let the word of Christ dwell in you richly" (Col 3:16).

The Publishers

GENESIS

G enesis stands as the introduction to the entire Bible and contains three main premises. It proclaims that God created a perfect world (1:1–2:25). It explains why that perfect world is now a mess (2:4–11:26). And it describes how God began a restoration process that continues through the Book of Revelation (11:27–50:26).

The book is organized around a simple Hebrew phrase, *'elle toledot*, which is translated in a variety of ways, including "These are the generations of," "This is the account of," and "This is the record of." Thus the repetition that exists in Hebrew often gets lost in our English translations (see 2:4; 5:1; 6:9; 10:1; 11:10, 27; 25:12, 19; 36:1, 9; 37:2). A simple way to translate the phrase is "This is what became of." As such, the first part of the book is a preface that briefly describes how God spoke the world into existence. The significance of the phrase is evident when we paraphrase Genesis 2:4 as "This is what became of the heavens and the earth" and see that the rest of the *'elle toledot* section describes how the sin of Adam and Eve (which we call *the fall*) affected the world. Subsequently the author used the phrase to mark a new section as he traced his narrative.

In the process the book outlines failure after failure of humanity, first corporately (through ch. 11), and then individually as God chose Abraham (chs. 12ff.) to begin a family and a nation that would eventually produce Jesus Christ and thus provide a means of restoration for the world. The overall picture is one of human unfaithfulness contrasted with God's faithfulness. Genesis focuses on four generations: Abraham, who believed God and obeyed God's call; his son Isaac; his grandson Jacob; and his great-grandsons, Jacob's twelve sons from whom the twelve tribes of Israel came. The book ends with this young nation incubating in Egypt, isolated from the corrupting influence of the various pagan tribes that had settled in the land God promised to Abraham (see the account of Judah in ch. 38).

THE CREATION OF THE WORLD

1 In the beginning God created the heavens and the earth. ² Now the earth was without shape and empty, and darkness was over the surface of the watery deep, but the Spirit of God was moving over the surface of the water. ³ God said, "Let there be light." And there was light! ⁴ God saw that the light was good, so God separated the light from the darkness. ⁵ God called the light "day" and the darkness "night." There was evening, and there was morning, marking the first day.

⁶ God said, "Let there be an expanse in the midst of the waters and let it separate water from water." ⁷ So God made the expanse and separated the water under the expanse from the water above it. It was so. ⁸ God called the expanse "sky." There was evening, and there was morning, a second day.

⁹ God said, "Let the water under the sky be gathered to one place and let dry ground appear." It was so. ¹⁰ God called the dry ground "land" and the gathered waters he called "seas." God saw that it was good.

¹¹ God said, "Let the land produce vegetation: plants yielding seeds and trees on the land bearing fruit with seed in it, according to their kinds." It was so. ¹² The land produced vegetation—plants yielding seeds according to their kinds, and trees bearing fruit with seed in it according to their kinds. God saw that it was good. ¹³ There was evening, and there was morning, a third day.

¹⁴ God said, "Let there be lights in the expanse of the sky to separate the day from the night, and let them be signs to indicate seasons and days and years, ¹⁵ and let them serve as lights in the expanse of the sky to give light on the earth." It was so. ¹⁶ God made two great lights—the greater light to rule over the day and the lesser light to rule over the night. He made the stars also. ¹⁷ God placed the lights in the expanse of the sky to shine on the earth, ¹⁸ to preside over the day and the night, and to separate the light from the darkness. God saw that it was good. ¹⁹ There was evening, and there was morning, a fourth day.

²⁰ God said, "Let the water swarm with swarms of living creatures and let birds fly above the earth across the expanse

CONTEMPLATE

Genesis 1:1–2

READ. Read the passage slowly. What about this portion of the creation narrative captures your attention: "In the beginning," "God created," "the earth was without shape and empty," or "the Spirit of God was moving"? Repeat it silently to yourself.

MEDITATE. Try to imagine the nothingness that existed before the creation of the universe. Which characteristics of God do these verses reveal? How are these characteristics still visible today?

PRAY. After experiencing the wonder of the first two verses of His Word, ask God's Spirit to speak to you. Then praise Him for His glorious creation of the heavens and the earth.

CONTEMPLATE. After praying, rest in God's presence. If time allows, go for a walk in His creation, and breathe in the presence of your Creator.

of the sky." 21God created the great sea creatures and every living and moving thing with which the water swarmed, according to their kinds, and every winged bird according to its kind. God saw that it was good. 22God blessed them and said, "Be fruitful and multiply and fill the water in the seas, and let the birds multiply on the earth." 23There was evening, and there was morning, a fifth day.

24God said, "Let the land produce living creatures according to their kinds: cattle, creeping things, and wild animals, each according to its kind." It was so. 25God made the wild animals according to their kinds, the cattle according to their kinds, and all the creatures that creep along the ground according to their kinds. God saw that it was good.

26Then God said, "Let us make humankind in our image, after our likeness, so they may rule over the fish of the sea and the birds of the air, over the cattle, and over all the earth, and over all the creatures that move on the earth."

27   God created humankind in his own image,
        in the image of God he created them,
        male and female he created them.

28God blessed them and said to them, "Be fruitful and multiply! Fill the earth and subdue it! Rule over the fish of the sea and the birds of the air and every creature that moves on the ground." 29Then God said, "I now give you every seed-bearing plant on the face of the entire earth and every tree that has fruit with seed in it. They will be yours for food. 30And to all the animals of the earth, and to every bird of the air, and to all the creatures that move on the ground—everything that has living breath in it—I give every green plant for food." It was so.

31God saw all that he had made—and it was very good! There was evening, and there was morning, the sixth day.

2 The heavens and the earth were completed with everything that was in them. 2By the seventh day God finished the work that he had been doing, and he ceased on the seventh day all the work that he had been doing. 3God blessed the seventh day and made it holy because on it he ceased all the work that he had been doing in creation.

PICTURE IT

Genesis 1:3–25

PICTURE. Imagine standing with God as He speaks creation into existence. How awed are you to see light for the first time? Describe what you see when God creates the land and the sea. What emotions do you feel when you see plants appear? Think about the creativity involved as God makes birds, fish, reptiles, and animals to inhabit the earth. Which one is your favorite? Which day holds the most amazement for you, and why? How does God show He is pleased with His creation (v. 25)?

PRAY. Ask God for the eyes to see the wonder of His creation, today and every day.

PRAYING SCRIPTURE

Genesis 1:26–31

As you read this passage, thank God for making all men and women in His image. Meditate on what that means in relation to your worth and identity. Ask God to help you treat other people with the love and dignity He shows you.

Next, thank God for the blessings He gave to humanity (v. 28). God proclaimed that the material world He created was good (v. 31). Notice in these verses the specific ways God has provided for our well-being. Then thank God for all the ways He has blessed your life—perhaps make a list!

God also gave us an opportunity to participate in His purposes. In Genesis 1:28, we see a short list of responsibilities. Notice the verbs used in this verse. How can we fulfill these roles in our daily lives?

THE CREATION OF MAN AND WOMAN

⁴ This is the account of the heavens and the earth when they were created—when the LORD God made the earth and heavens.

⁵ Now no shrub of the field had yet grown on the earth, and no plant of the field had yet sprouted, for the LORD God had not caused it to rain on the earth, and there was no man to cultivate the ground. ⁶ Springs would well up from the earth and water the whole surface of the ground. ⁷ The LORD God formed the man from the soil of the ground and breathed into his nostrils the breath of life, and the man became a living being.

⁸ The LORD God planted an orchard in the east, in Eden; and there he placed the man he had formed. ⁹ The LORD God made all kinds of trees grow from the soil, every tree that was pleasing to look at and good for food. (Now the tree of life and the tree of the knowledge of good and evil were in the middle of the orchard.)

¹⁰ Now a river flows from Eden to water the orchard, and from there it divides into four headstreams. ¹¹ The name of the first is Pishon; it runs through the entire land of Havilah, where there is gold. ¹² (The gold of that land is pure; pearls and lapis lazuli are also there.) ¹³ The name of the second river is Gihon; it runs through the entire land of Cush. ¹⁴ The name of the third river is Tigris; it runs along the east side of Assyria. The fourth river is the Euphrates.

¹⁵ The LORD God took the man and placed him in the orchard in Eden to care for it and to maintain it. ¹⁶ Then the LORD God commanded the man, "You may freely eat fruit from every tree of the orchard, ¹⁷ but you must not eat from the tree of the knowledge of good and evil, for when you eat from it you will surely die."

¹⁸ The LORD God said, "It is not good for the man to be alone. I will make a companion for him who corresponds to him." ¹⁹ The LORD God formed out of the ground every living animal of the field and every bird of the air. He brought them to the man to see what he would name them, and whatever the man called each living creature, that was its name. ²⁰ So

PICTURE IT

Genesis 2:8–17

PICTURE. Picture the orchard as it is described. Now imagine you're in it. As you stand in such an exquisite place, how do you feel? Do you grasp the grandeur of what is taking place? How beautiful and lush are the plants and land around you? What are you doing in the orchard as you take care of it (v. 15)? Picture the different trees. What does the fruit on the tree of life look like? What about the fruit on the other trees? Take in the smells, sounds, sights, tastes, and textures around you before you leave the orchard.

PRAY. Ask God to help you to remember the perfection in which humanity was placed. Thank Him for the beauty and splendor of His creation for your benefit.

PRAYING SCRIPTURE

Genesis 2:18–25

Thank God for designing us for relationships. What does it mean that the woman was like Adam (v. 18)? How should this truth shape marriage for the man and the woman?

Read Adam's reaction to seeing the woman for the first time (v. 23). What do you notice? Despite their differences, Adam and Eve were unashamed at this point in the story (v. 25). Imagine a life without shame, as Adam and Eve experienced. Pray against shame and doubt in your life today.

the man named all the animals, the birds of the air, and the living creatures of the field, but for Adam no companion who corresponded to him was found. ²¹ So the LORD God caused the man to fall into a deep sleep, and while he was asleep, he took part of the man's side and closed up the place with flesh. ²² Then the LORD God made a woman from the part he had taken out of the man, and he brought her to the man. ²³ Then the man said,

> "This one at last is bone of my bones
> and flesh of my flesh;
> this one will be called 'woman,'
> for she was taken out of man."

²⁴ That is why a man leaves his father and mother and unites with his wife, and they become one family. ²⁵ The man and his wife were both naked, but they were not ashamed.

THE TEMPTATION AND THE FALL

3 Now the serpent was shrewder than any of the wild animals that the LORD God had made. He said to the woman, "Is it really true that God said, 'You must not eat from any tree of the orchard'?" ² The woman said to the serpent, "We may eat of the fruit from the trees of the orchard; ³ but concerning the fruit of the tree that is in the middle of the orchard God said, 'You must not eat from it, and you must not touch it, or else you will die.'" ⁴ The serpent said to the woman, "Surely you will not die, ⁵ for God knows that when you eat from it your eyes will open and you will be like God, knowing good and evil."

⁶ When the woman saw that the tree produced fruit that was good for food, was attractive to the eye, and was desirable for making one wise, she took some of its fruit and ate it. She also gave some of it to her husband who was with her, and he ate it. ⁷ Then the eyes of both of them opened, and they knew they were naked; so they sewed fig leaves together and made coverings for themselves.

CONTEMPLATE

Genesis 3:1–13

READ. Take your time reading this section. As the story unfolds, note where you react the most. Which passage or phrase speaks to you? Is it the question posed to Eve in verse 1? The serpent's response in verses 4–5?

MEDITATE. How often does the Enemy deceive you with his craftiness? What can you ask the Spirit to do in a moment of temptation (1 Cor 10:13)? What does the passage or phrase you chose show you about your Enemy?

PRAY. In what area are you being tempted? Ask God to keep you far from temptation and the evil one (Matt 6:13). Pray that you would be quick to repent when you are led astray.

CONTEMPLATE. Now consider Christ's life, death, and resurrection. His perfect obedience conquered the power of sin that entered the world through Adam and Eve's rebellion. Choose to live in that freedom today (Gal 5:1).

THE JUDGMENT ORACLES OF GOD AT THE FALL

⁸ Then the man and his wife heard the sound of the LORD God moving about in the orchard at the breezy time of the day, and they hid from the LORD God among the trees of the orchard. ⁹ But the LORD God called to the man and said to him, "Where are you?" ¹⁰ The man replied, "I heard you moving about in the orchard, and I was afraid because I was naked, so I hid." ¹¹ And the LORD God said, "Who told you that you were naked? Did you eat from the tree that I commanded you not to eat from?" ¹² The man said, "The woman whom you gave me, she gave me some fruit from the tree and I ate it." ¹³ So the LORD God said to the woman, "What is this you have done?" And the woman replied, "The serpent tricked me, and I ate."

¹⁴ The LORD God said to the serpent,

"Because you have done this,
cursed are you above all the cattle
and all the living creatures of the field!
On your belly you will crawl
and dust you will eat all the days of your life.
15   And I will put hostility between you and the woman
and between your offspring and her offspring;
he will strike your head,
and you will strike his heel."

¹⁶ To the woman he said,

"I will greatly increase your labor pains;
with pain you will give birth to children.
You will want to control your husband,
but he will dominate you."

¹⁷ But to Adam he said,

"Because you obeyed your wife
and ate from the tree about which I commanded you,
'You must not eat from it,'
the ground is cursed because of you;
in painful toil you will eat of it all the days of your life.
18   It will produce thorns and thistles for you,
but you will eat the grain of the field.

JOURNAL

Genesis 3:16–24

REFLECT AND WRITE.

- What were sin's consequences for the woman? How are these relevant today?

- What curses did Adam experience? Describe these curses in today's language.

- What does it mean that we will return to dust (see v. 19)?

- How does Genesis 3 illustrate your need for a Savior?

- How might life be different today if Adam and Eve had not sinned?

19   By the sweat of your brow you will eat food
      until you return to the ground,
      for out of it you were taken;
      for you are dust, and to dust you will return."

²⁰ The man named his wife Eve, because she was the mother of all the living. ²¹ The LORD God made garments from skin for Adam and his wife, and clothed them. ²² And the LORD God said, "Now that the man has become like one of us, knowing good and evil, he must not be allowed to stretch out his hand and take also from the tree of life and eat, and live forever." ²³ So the LORD God expelled him from the orchard in Eden to cultivate the ground from which he had been taken. ²⁴ When he drove the man out, he placed on the eastern side of the orchard in Eden angelic sentries who used the flame of a whirling sword to guard the way to the tree of life.

THE STORY OF CAIN AND ABEL

4 Now the man was intimate with his wife Eve, and she became pregnant and gave birth to Cain. Then she said, "I have created a man just as the LORD did!" ² Then she gave birth to his brother Abel. Abel took care of the flocks, while Cain cultivated the ground.

³ At the designated time Cain brought some of the fruit of the ground for an offering to the LORD. ⁴ But Abel brought some of the firstborn of his flock—even the fattest of them. And the LORD was pleased with Abel and his offering, ⁵ but with Cain and his offering he was not pleased. So Cain became very angry, and his expression was downcast.

⁶ Then the LORD said to Cain, "Why are you angry, and why is your expression downcast? ⁷ Is it not true that if you do what is right, you will be fine? But if you do not do what is right, sin is crouching at the door. It desires to dominate you, but you must subdue it."

⁸ Cain said to his brother Abel, "Let's go out to the field." While they were in the field, Cain attacked his brother Abel and killed him.

 CONTEMPLATE

Genesis 4:1–14

READ. Read this passage of Scripture twice. The first time, take note of its main theme. The second time, consider either Cain's and Abel's offerings (vv. 3–4) or the Lord's response to Cain's attitude (vv. 5–7). Allow it to speak to you.

MEDITATE. Why did God consider Abel righteous (Heb 11:4)? What does God's response reveal about Cain's heart and the nature of his gift? Are you holding anything back from God?

PRAY. Ask God to reveal any area of your life in which you may be withholding thanksgiving He is due. Respond with a thankful heart following any revelation you receive.

CONTEMPLATE. Quiet yourself and rest a moment in the assurance of God's continual provision and constant love for you and for all His creation.

⁹ Then the LORD said to Cain, "Where is your brother Abel?" And he replied, "I don't know! Am I my brother's guardian?" ¹⁰ But the LORD said, "What have you done? The voice of your brother's blood is crying out to me from the ground! ¹¹ So now you are banished from the ground, which has opened its mouth to receive your brother's blood from your hand. ¹² When you try to cultivate the ground it will no longer yield its best for you. You will be a homeless wanderer on the earth."

¹³ Then Cain said to the LORD, "My punishment is too great to endure! ¹⁴ Look, you are driving me off the land today, and I must hide from your presence. I will be a homeless wanderer on the earth; whoever finds me will kill me!" ¹⁵ But the LORD said to him, "All right then, if anyone kills Cain, Cain will be avenged seven times as much." Then the LORD put a special mark on Cain so that no one who found him would strike him down. ¹⁶ So Cain went out from the presence of the LORD and lived in the land of Nod, east of Eden.

THE BEGINNING OF CIVILIZATION

¹⁷ Cain was intimate with his wife, and she became pregnant and gave birth to Enoch. Cain was building a city, and he named the city after his son Enoch. ¹⁸ To Enoch was born Irad, and Irad was the father of Mehujael. Mehujael was the father of Methushael, and Methushael was the father of Lamech.

¹⁹ Lamech took two wives for himself; the name of the first was Adah, and the name of the second was Zillah. ²⁰ Adah gave birth to Jabal; he was the first of those who live in tents and keep livestock. ²¹ The name of his brother was Jubal; he was the first of all who play the harp and the flute. ²² Now Zillah also gave birth to Tubal-Cain, who heated metal and shaped all kinds of tools made of bronze and iron. The sister of Tubal-Cain was Naamah.

²³ Lamech said to his wives,

"Adah and Zillah, listen to me!
You wives of Lamech, hear my words!
I have killed a man for wounding me,
a young man for hurting me.
²⁴ If Cain is to be avenged seven times as much,
then Lamech seventy-seven times!"

PRAYING SCRIPTURE

Genesis 4:16–24

Understanding the meaning of biblical genealogies can be difficult, but here we see God working to preserve godly generations. At the heart of a family is marriage. Genesis 4:19 shows that the sanctity of marriage between one man and one woman can easily be adulterated. Pray that God would preserve His design for marriage.

After Cain killed his brother, Abel (Gen 4:8), God punished him. If, however, someone killed Cain, vengeance on that person would be great (Gen 4:15). Generations later, Lamech admitted he had killed a young man. In remorse, Lamech said he deserved to be avenged even more than Cain (vv. 23–24). Now read Matthew 18:21–22 and notice how Jesus turned this passage upside down. Thank God for His forgiveness, which sets us free.

²⁵ And Adam was intimate with his wife again, and she gave birth to a son. She named him Seth, saying, "God has given me another child in place of Abel because Cain killed him." ²⁶ And a son was also born to Seth, whom he named Enosh. At that time people began to worship the LORD.

FROM ADAM TO NOAH

5 This is the record of the family line of Adam.
When God created humankind, he made them in the likeness of God. ² He created them male and female; when they were created, he blessed them and named them "humankind."

³ When Adam had lived 130 years he fathered a son in his own likeness, according to his image, and he named him Seth. ⁴ The length of time Adam lived after he became the father of Seth was 800 years; during this time he had other sons and daughters. ⁵ The entire lifetime of Adam was 930 years, and then he died.

⁶ When Seth had lived 105 years, he became the father of Enosh. ⁷ Seth lived 807 years after he became the father of Enosh, and he had other sons and daughters. ⁸ The entire lifetime of Seth was 912 years, and then he died.

⁹ When Enosh had lived 90 years, he became the father of Kenan. ¹⁰ Enosh lived 815 years after he became the father of Kenan, and he had other sons and daughters. ¹¹ The entire lifetime of Enosh was 905 years, and then he died.

¹² When Kenan had lived 70 years, he became the father of Mahalalel. ¹³ Kenan lived 840 years after he became the father of Mahalalel, and he had other sons and daughters. ¹⁴ The entire lifetime of Kenan was 910 years, and then he died.

¹⁵ When Mahalalel had lived 65 years, he became the father of Jared. ¹⁶ Mahalalel lived 830 years after he became the father of Jared, and he had other sons and daughters. ¹⁷ The entire lifetime of Mahalalel was 895 years, and then he died.

¹⁸ When Jared had lived 162 years, he became the father of Enoch. ¹⁹ Jared lived 800 years after he became the father of Enoch, and he had other sons and daughters. ²⁰ The entire lifetime of Jared was 962 years, and then he died.

CONTEMPLATE

Genesis 4:25–26

READ. Read the passage, paying special attention to verse 26: "At that time people began to worship the LORD." Allow the phrase to take root in your heart.

MEDITATE. What is significant about this moment in Genesis? How can you call on God in your circumstances today? By which name will you call on Him: God with Us, Savior, Redeemer, Prince of Peace?

PRAY. Pray that instead of leaning on your own understanding and strength, you will be quick to call on the name of the Lord, no matter the trials or successes you may face.

CONTEMPLATE. Rest in His presence. He is the God of peace, all comfort, loyal love, and grace (Ps 143:8; 2 Cor 1:3; Eph 2:8–9; 2 Thess 3:16).

 JOURNAL

Genesis 5:1–29

REFLECT AND WRITE.

• Why is this genealogy important for the Genesis narrative?

• In whose image were Adam and Eve formed (see Gen 1:27)? In whose likeness and image was Seth formed (see v. 3)? Why is there a difference?

• Compare Adam's legacy (see vv. 3–5) with Enoch's legacy (see vv. 21–24).

• How was Noah's name (see v. 29) fitting for his future role (see Gen 6–8)?

²¹When Enoch had lived 65 years, he became the father of Methuselah. ²²After he became the father of Methuselah, Enoch walked with God for 300 years, and he had other sons and daughters. ²³The entire lifetime of Enoch was 365 years. ²⁴Enoch walked with God, and then he disappeared because God took him away.

²⁵When Methuselah had lived 187 years, he became the father of Lamech. ²⁶Methuselah lived 782 years after he became the father of Lamech, and he had other sons and daughters. ²⁷The entire lifetime of Methuselah was 969 years, and then he died.

²⁸When Lamech had lived 182 years, he had a son. ²⁹He named him Noah, saying, "This one will bring us comfort from our labor and from the painful toil of our hands because of the ground that the LORD has cursed." ³⁰Lamech lived 595 years after he became the father of Noah, and he had other sons and daughters. ³¹The entire lifetime of Lamech was 777 years, and then he died.

³²After Noah was 500 years old, he became the father of Shem, Ham, and Japheth.

GOD'S GRIEF OVER HUMANKIND'S WICKEDNESS

6 When humankind began to multiply on the face of the earth, and daughters were born to them, ²the sons of God saw that the daughters of humankind were beautiful. Thus they took wives for themselves from any they chose. ³So the LORD said, "My Spirit will not remain in humankind indefinitely, since they are mortal. They will remain for 120 more years."

⁴The Nephilim were on the earth in those days (and also after this) when the sons of God would sleep with the daughters of humankind, who gave birth to their children. They were the mighty heroes of old, the famous men.

⁵But the LORD saw that the wickedness of humankind had become great on the earth. Every inclination of the thoughts of their minds was only evil all the time. ⁶The LORD regretted that he had made humankind on the earth, and he was highly offended. ⁷So the LORD said, "I will wipe humankind,

CONTEMPLATE

Genesis 6:1–8

READ. Read the passage carefully. Look for a phrase that speaks to you. Is it the Lord's observation in verse 5 or the evidence of His grace in verse 8? Repeat the phrase, allowing it to sink in.

MEDITATE. Do you see evidence that humanity's wickedness is "great on the earth" today (v. 5)? How can you put evil far from your heart? How was Noah different from wicked people? How can you look like Christ in a world that often looks depraved?

PRAY. Ask God to remind you of His perfect love for you. Pray for specific people to repent and turn to the Lord. Pray that you would continue to walk closely with Christ.

CONTEMPLATE. Be silent in God's presence. Rest in Him, knowing His grace is sufficient for you (2 Cor 12:9–10).

whom I have created, from the face of the earth—everything from humankind to animals, including creatures that move on the ground and birds of the air, for I regret that I have made them."

8 But Noah found favor in the sight of the LORD.

THE JUDGMENT OF THE FLOOD

9 This is the account of Noah.

Noah was a godly man; he was blameless among his contemporaries. He walked with God. 10 Noah had three sons: Shem, Ham, and Japheth.

11 The earth was ruined in the sight of God; the earth was filled with violence. 12 God saw the earth, and indeed it was ruined, for all living creatures on the earth were sinful. 13 So God said to Noah, "I have decided that all living creatures must die, for the earth is filled with violence because of them. Now I am about to destroy them and the earth. 14 Make for yourself an ark of cypress wood. Make rooms in the ark, and cover it with pitch inside and out. 15 This is how you should make it: The ark is to be 450 feet long, 75 feet wide, and 45 feet high. 16 Make a roof for the ark and finish it, leaving 18 inches from the top. Put a door in the side of the ark, and make lower, middle, and upper decks. 17 I am about to bring floodwaters on the earth to destroy from under the sky all the living creatures that have the breath of life in them. Everything that is on the earth will die, 18 but I will confirm my covenant with you. You will enter the ark—you, your sons, your wife, and your sons' wives with you. 19 You must bring into the ark two of every kind of living creature from all flesh, male and female, to keep them alive with you. 20 Of the birds after their kinds, and of the cattle after their kinds, and of every creeping thing of the ground after its kind, two of every kind will come to you so you can keep them alive. 21 And you must take for yourself every kind of food that is eaten, and gather it together. It will be food for you and for them."

22 And Noah did all that God commanded him—he did indeed.

PRAYING
SCRIPTURE

Genesis 6:11–22

Reading this passage might seem like reading today's news. In the story of creation in Genesis 1, God was pleased by His creation of the world. So how did things go so wrong? What are the root causes of sin? In this passage, God brought judgment on evil. But He established a new beginning by sparing the lives of Noah and his family. How has God given you new beginnings when you needed them? Thank Him; then ask Him to help you bring light into the darkness.

7 The LORD said to Noah, "Come into the ark, you and all your household, for I consider you godly among this generation. ²You must take with you seven pairs of every kind of clean animal, the male and its mate, two of every kind of unclean animal, the male and its mate, ³and also seven pairs of every kind of bird in the sky, male and female, to preserve their offspring on the face of the entire earth. ⁴For in seven days I will cause it to rain on the earth for forty days and forty nights, and I will wipe from the face of the ground every living thing that I have made."

⁵And Noah did all that the LORD commanded him.

⁶Noah was 600 years old when the floodwaters engulfed the earth. ⁷Noah entered the ark along with his sons, his wife, and his sons' wives because of the floodwaters. ⁸Pairs of clean animals, of unclean animals, of birds, and of everything that creeps along the ground, ⁹male and female, came into the ark to Noah, just as God had commanded him. ¹⁰And after seven days the floodwaters engulfed the earth.

¹¹In the six hundredth year of Noah's life, in the second month, on the seventeenth day of the month—on that day all the fountains of the great deep burst open and the floodgates of the heavens were opened. ¹²And the rain fell on the earth forty days and forty nights.

¹³On that very day Noah entered the ark, accompanied by his sons Shem, Ham, and Japheth, along with his wife and his sons' three wives. ¹⁴They entered, along with every living creature after its kind, every animal after its kind, every creeping thing that creeps on the earth after its kind, and every bird after its kind, everything with wings. ¹⁵Pairs of all creatures that have the breath of life came into the ark to Noah. ¹⁶Those that entered were male and female, just as God commanded him. Then the LORD shut him in.

¹⁷The flood engulfed the earth for forty days. As the waters increased, they lifted the ark and raised it above the earth. ¹⁸The waters completely overwhelmed the earth, and the ark floated on the surface of the waters. ¹⁹The waters completely inundated the earth so that even all the high mountains under the entire sky were covered. ²⁰The

JOURNAL

Genesis 7:1–5, 17–24

REFLECT AND WRITE.

- Why would Noah need seven each of all clean animals and only two each of unclean animals?

- What kind of damage and long-term effects would weeks of extended rain have had on the earth?

- How was it just for God, who had once called creation "very good" (Gen 1:31), to destroy almost everything He had created?

waters rose more than 20 feet above the mountains. [21] And all living things that moved on the earth died, including the birds, domestic animals, wild animals, all the creatures that swarm over the earth, and all humankind. [22] Everything on dry land that had the breath of life in its nostrils died. [23] So the LORD destroyed every living thing that was on the surface of the ground, including people, animals, creatures that creep along the ground, and birds of the sky. They were wiped off the earth. Only Noah and those who were with him in the ark survived. [24] The waters prevailed over the earth for 150 days.

8 But God remembered Noah and all the wild animals and domestic animals that were with him in the ark. God caused a wind to blow over the earth and the waters receded. [2] The fountains of the deep and the floodgates of heaven were closed, and the rain stopped falling from the sky. [3] The waters kept receding steadily from the earth, so that they had gone down by the end of the 150 days. [4] On the seventeenth day of the seventh month, the ark came to rest on one of the mountains of Ararat. [5] The waters kept on receding until the tenth month. On the first day of the tenth month, the tops of the mountains became visible.

[6] At the end of forty days, Noah opened the window he had made in the ark [7] and sent out a raven; it kept flying back and forth until the waters had dried up on the earth.

[8] Then Noah sent out a dove to see if the waters had receded from the surface of the ground. [9] The dove could not find a resting place for its feet because water still covered the surface of the entire earth, and so it returned to Noah in the ark. He stretched out his hand, took the dove, and brought it back into the ark. [10] He waited seven more days and then sent out the dove again from the ark. [11] When the dove returned to him in the evening, there was a freshly plucked olive leaf in its beak! Noah knew that the waters had receded from the earth. [12] He waited another seven days and sent the dove out again, but it did not return to him this time.

CONTEMPLATE

Genesis 8:1–12, 15–19

READ. Read these verses twice. Look for words or phrases that catch your attention. Take note of all that God remembered in verse 1. Repeat any phrase that speaks to you.

MEDITATE. What about the phrase you chose speaks to your heart? Notice that when God remembers someone or something, He acts on its behalf. How does God remember you? How can this encourage you to abide more in who Christ is?

PRAY. Now turn your focus toward prayer. Maintain a listening posture and allow God to speak to you. Thank Him that He has chosen you (Eph 1:4–6), remembers you, and acts on your behalf.

CONTEMPLATE. Choose a memory that demonstrates God's work on your behalf. Revisit each detail. Linger a moment in His faithful love.

¹³ In Noah's six hundred and first year, in the first day of the first month, the waters had dried up from the earth, and Noah removed the covering from the ark and saw that the surface of the ground was dry. ¹⁴ And by the twenty-seventh day of the second month the earth was dry.

¹⁵ Then God spoke to Noah and said, ¹⁶ "Come out of the ark, you, your wife, your sons, and your sons' wives with you. ¹⁷ Bring out with you all the living creatures that are with you. Bring out every living thing, including the birds, animals, and every creeping thing that creeps on the earth. Let them increase and be fruitful and multiply on the earth!"

¹⁸ Noah went out along with his sons, his wife, and his sons' wives. ¹⁹ Every living creature, every creeping thing, every bird, and everything that moves on the earth went out of the ark in their groups.

²⁰ Noah built an altar to the LORD. He then took some of every kind of clean animal and clean bird and offered burnt offerings on the altar. ²¹ And the LORD smelled the soothing aroma and said to himself, "I will never again curse the ground because of humankind, even though the inclination of their minds is evil from childhood on. I will never again destroy everything that lives, as I have just done.

²² "While the earth continues to exist,
    planting time and harvest,
    cold and heat,
    summer and winter,
    and day and night will not cease."

GOD'S COVENANT WITH HUMANKIND THROUGH NOAH

9 Then God blessed Noah and his sons and said to them, "Be fruitful and multiply and fill the earth. ² Every living creature of the earth and every bird of the sky will be terrified of you. Everything that creeps on the ground and all the fish of the sea are under your authority. ³ You may eat any moving thing that lives. As I gave you the green plants, I now give you everything.

PRAYING
SCRIPTURE

Genesis 8:20–21

After God saved Noah's family from the flood, Noah offered sacrifices. In your view, what was in Noah's heart and mind? Today, people in western cultures don't typically build altars and offer sacrifices. How can you worship God with the same love Noah had for Him?

In verse 21, God said He would never again destroy the entire world. Praise God for His faithfulness to humanity, even though our hearts often turn away from Him. Praise Him for His faithfulness to you.

4 "But you must not eat meat with its life (that is, its blood) in it. 5 For your lifeblood I will surely exact punishment, from every living creature I will exact punishment. From each person I will exact punishment for the life of the individual since the man was his relative.

6   "Whoever sheds human blood,
by other humans
must his blood be shed;
for in God's image
God has made humankind.

7 "But as for you, be fruitful and multiply; increase abundantly on the earth and multiply on it."

8 God said to Noah and his sons, 9 "Look. I now confirm my covenant with you and your descendants after you 10 and with every living creature that is with you, including the birds, the domestic animals, and every living creature of the earth with you, all those that came out of the ark with you—every living creature of the earth. 11 I confirm my covenant with you: Never again will all living things be wiped out by the waters of a flood; never again will a flood destroy the earth."

12 And God said, "This is the guarantee of the covenant I am making with you and every living creature with you, a covenant for all subsequent generations: 13 I will place my rainbow in the clouds, and it will become a guarantee of the covenant between me and the earth. 14 Whenever I bring clouds over the earth and the rainbow appears in the clouds, 15 then I will remember my covenant with you and with all living creatures of all kinds. Never again will the waters become a flood and destroy all living things. 16 When the rainbow is in the clouds, I will notice it and remember the perpetual covenant between God and all living creatures of all kinds that are on the earth."

17 So God said to Noah, "This is the guarantee of the covenant that I am confirming between me and all living things that are on the earth."

PICTURE IT

Genesis 9:8–17

PICTURE. Imagine making a covenant with God Almighty. Imagine God saying He desires to establish a covenant with you and your family. After all you witnessed and endured on the ark, how do you feel when you hear these words: "Never again will all living things be wiped out by the waters of a flood" (v. 11)? Do you believe it? Imagine seeing a rainbow for the first time. What feelings and thoughts overcome you? How does this give you hope for the covenant God speaks of (v. 16)?

PRAY. Thank God for His promise that extends past Noah to you today. Ask God to remind you each time you see a rainbow of the covenant of grace He made. Praise Him for His grace and abundant love.

THE CURSE ON CANAAN

18 The sons of Noah who came out of the ark were Shem, Ham, and Japheth. (Now Ham was the father of Canaan.) 19 These were the three sons of Noah, and from them the whole earth was populated.

20 Noah, a man of the soil, began to plant a vineyard. 21 When he drank some of the wine, he got drunk and uncovered himself inside his tent. 22 Ham, the father of Canaan, saw his father's nakedness and told his two brothers who were outside. 23 Shem and Japheth took the garment and placed it on their shoulders. Then they walked in backwards and covered up their father's nakedness. Their faces were turned the other way so they did not see their father's nakedness.

24 When Noah awoke from his drunken stupor he learned what his youngest son had done to him. 25 So he said,

"Cursed be Canaan!
The lowest of slaves
he will be to his brothers."

26 He also said,

"Worthy of praise is the LORD, the God of Shem!
May Canaan be the slave of Shem!
27   May God enlarge Japheth's territory and numbers!
May he live in the tents of Shem
and may Canaan be the slave of Japheth!"

28 After the flood Noah lived 350 years. 29 The entire lifetime of Noah was 950 years, and then he died.

THE TABLE OF NATIONS

10 This is the account of Noah's sons: Shem, Ham, and Japheth. Sons were born to them after the flood.

2 The sons of Japheth were Gomer, Magog, Madai, Javan, Tubal, Meshech, and Tiras. 3 The sons of Gomer were Ashkenaz, Riphath, and Togarmah. 4 The sons of Javan were Elishah, Tarshish, the Kittim, and the Dodanim. 5 From these the coastlands of the nations were separated into their lands,

 CONTEMPLATE

Genesis 9:18–29

READ. Ask God to reveal Himself through His Word. Then read this passage, searching for a word or phrase that catches your attention. Consider the blessings Noah spoke over Shem and Japheth for honoring him, the curse for Ham's dishonor, or the duration of Noah's life (vv. 25–28).

MEDITATE. Why did the phrase you chose catch your eye? How does God exalt the humble (Matt 23:12), and what can you learn from this? In what way does Noah demonstrate faithfulness and righteousness?

PRAY. Pray that you will live a lifetime of faithful service and obedience to God. Ask Him to reveal areas of your life in which you lack humility. Then confess it as sin. Ask God to keep you mindful of your heart in those areas.

CONTEMPLATE. Take a moment to be still. Read Micah 6:8 and commit to live its words in your life today.

every one according to its language, according to their families, by their nations.

6 The sons of Ham were Cush, Mizraim, Put, and Canaan. 7 The sons of Cush were Seba, Havilah, Sabtah, Raamah, and Sabteca. The sons of Raamah were Sheba and Dedan.

8 Cush was the father of Nimrod; he began to be a valiant warrior on the earth. 9 He was a mighty hunter before the LORD. (That is why it is said, "Like Nimrod, a mighty hunter before the LORD.") 10 The primary regions of his kingdom were Babel, Erech, Akkad, and Calneh in the land of Shinar. 11 From that land he went to Assyria, where he built Nineveh, Rehoboth Ir, Calah, 12 and Resen, which is between Nineveh and the great city Calah.

13 Mizraim was the father of the Ludites, Anamites, Lehabites, Naphtuhites, 14 Pathrusites, Casluhites (from whom the Philistines came), and Caphtorites.

15 Canaan was the father of Sidon his firstborn, Heth, 16 the Jebusites, Amorites, Girgashites, 17 Hivites, Arkites, Sinites, 18 Arvadites, Zemarites, and Hamathites. Eventually the families of the Canaanites were scattered 19 and the borders of Canaan extended from Sidon all the way to Gerar as far as Gaza, and all the way to Sodom, Gomorrah, Admah, and Zeboyim, as far as Lasha. 20 These are the sons of Ham, according to their families, according to their languages, by their lands, and by their nations.

21 And sons were also born to Shem (the older brother of Japheth), the father of all the sons of Eber.

22 The sons of Shem were Elam, Asshur, Arphaxad, Lud, and Aram. 23 The sons of Aram were Uz, Hul, Gether, and Mash. 24 Arphaxad was the father of Shelah, and Shelah was the father of Eber. 25 Two sons were born to Eber: One was named Peleg because in his days the earth was divided, and his brother's name was Joktan. 26 Joktan was the father of Almodad, Sheleph, Hazarmaveth, Jerah, 27 Hadoram, Uzal, Diklah, 28 Obal, Abimael, Sheba, 29 Ophir, Havilah, and Jobab. All these were sons of Joktan. 30 Their dwelling place was from Mesha all the way to Sephar in the eastern hills. 31 These are

JOURNAL

Genesis 10:1–12, 15–22, 32

REFLECT AND WRITE.

- Which names look familiar in Noah's genealogy? What do you recall about any of these characters?

- Why is this genealogy so important in the biblical narrative?

- What do you know about any of the cities mentioned in verses 8–12 and 15–20? How do these cities fore-shadow the Tower of Babel (see Gen 11:1–9)?

the sons of Shem according to their families, according to their languages, by their lands, and according to their nations.

32 These are the families of the sons of Noah, according to their genealogies, by their nations, and from these the nations spread over the earth after the flood.

THE DISPERSION OF THE NATIONS AT BABEL

11 The whole earth had a common language and a common vocabulary. 2 When the people moved eastward, they found a plain in Shinar and settled there. 3 Then they said to one another, "Come, let's make bricks and bake them thoroughly." (They had brick instead of stone and tar instead of mortar.) 4 Then they said, "Come, let's build ourselves a city and a tower with its top in the heavens so that we may make a name for ourselves. Otherwise we will be scattered across the face of the entire earth."

5 But the LORD came down to see the city and the tower that the people had started building. 6 And the LORD said, "If as one people all sharing a common language they have begun to do this, then nothing they plan to do will be beyond them. 7 Come, let's go down and confuse their language so they won't be able to understand each other."

8 So the LORD scattered them from there across the face of the entire earth, and they stopped building the city. 9 That is why its name was called Babel—because there the LORD confused the language of the entire world, and from there the LORD scattered them across the face of the entire earth.

THE GENEALOGY OF SHEM

10 This is the account of Shem.

Shem was 100 years old when he became the father of Arphaxad, two years after the flood. 11 And after becoming the father of Arphaxad, Shem lived 500 years and had other sons and daughters.

12 When Arphaxad had lived 35 years, he became the father of Shelah. 13 And after he became the father of Shelah, Arphaxad lived 403 years and had other sons and daughters.

PICTURE IT

Genesis 11:1–9

PICTURE. Imagine you and everyone you know are journeying eastward together. You decide on a place to settle and begin building a city. Now picture the brick and asphalt tower you have created. How tall is it? What does it look like? What is your plan for the tower (read the first half of v. 4)? How does this plan contradict God's desire for you (Gen 1:28; 9:1, 7)? Imagine suddenly not being able to understand your family members, neighbors, or close friends. How do you feel knowing this scattering was part of God's plan? Picture the journey you and those you can communicate with take to settle into a new land.

PRAY. Talk to God about any "towers" you may be building that have more to do with making yourself great than they do with obeying God and making Him great.

14 When Shelah had lived 30 years, he became the father of Eber. 15 And after he became the father of Eber, Shelah lived 403 years and had other sons and daughters.

16 When Eber had lived 34 years, he became the father of Peleg. 17 And after he became the father of Peleg, Eber lived 430 years and had other sons and daughters.

18 When Peleg had lived 30 years, he became the father of Reu. 19 And after he became the father of Reu, Peleg lived 209 years and had other sons and daughters.

20 When Reu had lived 32 years, he became the father of Serug. 21 And after he became the father of Serug, Reu lived 207 years and had other sons and daughters.

22 When Serug had lived 30 years, he became the father of Nahor. 23 And after he became the father of Nahor, Serug lived 200 years and had other sons and daughters.

24 When Nahor had lived 29 years, he became the father of Terah. 25 And after he became the father of Terah, Nahor lived 119 years and had other sons and daughters.

26 When Terah had lived 70 years, he became the father of Abram, Nahor, and Haran.

THE RECORD OF TERAH

27 This is the account of Terah.

Terah became the father of Abram, Nahor, and Haran. And Haran became the father of Lot. 28 Haran died in the land of his birth, in Ur of the Chaldeans, while his father Terah was still alive. 29 And Abram and Nahor took wives for themselves. The name of Abram's wife was Sarai. And the name of Nahor's wife was Milcah; she was the daughter of Haran, who was the father of both Milcah and Iscah. 30 But Sarai was barren; she had no children.

31 Terah took his son Abram, his grandson Lot (the son of Haran), and his daughter-in-law Sarai, his son Abram's wife, and with them he set out from Ur of the Chaldeans to go to Canaan. When they came to Haran, they settled there. 32 The lifetime of Terah was 205 years, and he died in Haran.

CONTEMPLATE

Genesis 11:26–32

READ. As you read, note the descendants who emerge from the genealogy. Read the passage again slowly and find a name or place you can't overlook. Perhaps it's Abram, Sarai, Terah, or the land of Canaan.

MEDITATE. Based on what you know about this person or place already, why do you think it stood out to you?

PRAY. Ask the Spirit to connect the story God tells through the lives of the men and women of faith to His eternal truths. Ask the Father to help you live out those truths.

CONTEMPLATE. After praying, rest in the shadow of the Sovereign One (Ps 91:1). Like the men and women mentioned in today's passage, commit to be a person who makes an impact in the lives of those around you and who leaves a kingdom legacy.

THE OBEDIENCE OF ABRAM

12 Now the LORD said to Abram,
"Go out from your country, your relatives,
and your father's household
to the land that I will show you.
2 Then I will make you into a great
nation, and I will bless you,
and I will make your name great,
so that you will exemplify divine blessing.
3 I will bless those who bless you,
but the one who treats you lightly I must curse,
so that all the families of the earth may
receive blessing through you."

4 So Abram left, just as the LORD had told him to do, and Lot went with him. (Now Abram was 75 years old when he departed from Haran.) 5 And Abram took his wife Sarai, his nephew Lot, and all the possessions they had accumulated and the people they had acquired in Haran, and they left for the land of Canaan. They entered the land of Canaan. 6 Abram traveled through the land as far as the oak tree of Moreh at Shechem. (At that time the Canaanites were in the land.) 7 The LORD appeared to Abram and said, "To your descendants I will give this land." So Abram built an altar there to the LORD, who had appeared to him. 8 Then he moved from there to the hill country east of Bethel and pitched his tent, with Bethel on the west and Ai on the east. There he built an altar to the LORD and worshiped the LORD. 9 Abram continually journeyed by stages down to the Negev.

THE PROMISED BLESSING JEOPARDIZED

10 There was a famine in the land, so Abram went down to Egypt to stay for a while because the famine was severe. 11 As he approached Egypt, he said to his wife Sarai, "Look, I know that you are a beautiful woman. 12 When the Egyptians see you they will say, 'This is his wife.' Then they will kill me but will keep you alive. 13 So tell them you are my sister so that it may go well for me because of you and my life will be spared on account of you."

PRAYING SCRIPTURE

Genesis 12:1–3

As you read these verses, consider the reasons God wanted Abram to leave his country and family. Abram obeyed even though he didn't know where to go. Pray that God would help you obey His call, even when the path forward is unclear.

Next, pray that God would bless others through you as He blessed the nations through Abram. Think creatively about ways to be a blessing to those around you—verbally, financially, spiritually, physically, emotionally. Read also Matthew 28:18–20 and pray that God would help you, your family, and your church advance the gospel of God's grace into the nations.

CONTEMPLATE

Genesis 12:4–9

READ. Read the passage and allow yourself to stop and ask questions. Choose a phrase: "Abram left, just as the LORD had told him to do" (v. 4), "built an altar" (v. 8), or "Abram continually journeyed" (v. 9). Spend time repeating the phrase.

MEDITATE. What do you learn about Abram's obedience and journey in this passage? How do you anticipate that the Spirit will use these verses to speak to you?

PRAY. How can you affirm that you trust God's plan for your life and journey forward? Abram built altars both to remember and to thank God. Ask Him how to respond to all He has done.

CONTEMPLATE. Practice a moment of quiet reflection alone with your Lord.

¹⁴ When Abram entered Egypt, the Egyptians saw that the woman was very beautiful. ¹⁵ When Pharaoh's officials saw her, they praised her to Pharaoh. So Abram's wife was taken into the household of Pharaoh, ¹⁶ and he did treat Abram well on account of her. Abram received sheep and cattle, male donkeys, male servants, female servants, female donkeys, and camels.

¹⁷ But the LORD struck Pharaoh and his household with severe diseases because of Sarai, Abram's wife. ¹⁸ So Pharaoh summoned Abram and said, "What is this you have done to me? Why didn't you tell me that she was your wife? ¹⁹ Why did you say, 'She is my sister,' so that I took her to be my wife? Now, here is your wife. Take her and go!" ²⁰ Pharaoh gave his men orders about Abram, and so they expelled him, along with his wife and all his possessions.

ABRAM'S SOLUTION TO THE STRIFE

13 So Abram went up from Egypt into the Negev. He took his wife and all his possessions with him, as well as Lot. ² (Now Abram was very wealthy in livestock, silver, and gold.)

³ And he journeyed from place to place from the Negev as far as Bethel. He returned to the place where he had pitched his tent at the beginning, between Bethel and Ai. ⁴ This was the place where he had first built the altar, and there Abram worshiped the LORD.

⁵ Now Lot, who was traveling with Abram, also had flocks, herds, and tents. ⁶ But the land could not support them while they were living side by side. Because their possessions were so great, they were not able to live alongside one another. ⁷ So there were quarrels between Abram's herdsmen and Lot's herdsmen. (Now the Canaanites and the Perizzites were living in the land at that time.)

⁸ Abram said to Lot, "Let there be no quarreling between me and you, and between my herdsmen and your herdsmen, for we are close relatives. ⁹ Is not the whole land before you? Separate yourself now from me. If you go to the left, then I'll go to the right, but if you go to the right, then I'll go to the left."

JOURNAL

Genesis 12:10–20

REFLECT AND WRITE.

- What plan did Abram devise to stay alive in Egypt? What were the benefits and drawbacks of his plan?

- How did Pharaoh suffer from their plan (see v. 17)? How did he respond to Abram?

- How did the plagues allow God to fulfill His promise to make the descendants of Abram and Sarai into "a great nation" (Gen 12:2)?

JOURNAL

Genesis 13:5–9

REFLECT AND WRITE.

- Which verse speaks to you the most today? What might the Spirit want to say to you through this verse?

- Consider Abram's request for Lot to choose land separate from his own (see v. 9). How can you relate to or empathize with Abram in this decision?

¹⁰ Lot looked up and saw the whole region of the Jordan. He noticed that all of it was well watered (this was before the LORD obliterated Sodom and Gomorrah) like the garden of the LORD, like the land of Egypt, all the way to Zoar. ¹¹ Lot chose for himself the whole region of the Jordan and traveled toward the east.

So the relatives separated from each other. ¹² Abram settled in the land of Canaan, but Lot settled among the cities of the Jordan plain and pitched his tents next to Sodom. ¹³ (Now the people of Sodom were extremely wicked rebels against the LORD.)

¹⁴ After Lot had departed, the LORD said to Abram, "Look from the place where you stand to the north, south, east, and west. ¹⁵ I will give all the land that you see to you and your descendants forever. ¹⁶ And I will make your descendants like the dust of the earth, so that if anyone is able to count the dust of the earth, then your descendants also can be counted. ¹⁷ Get up and walk throughout the land, for I will give it to you."

¹⁸ So Abram moved his tents and went to live by the oaks of Mamre in Hebron, and he built an altar to the LORD there.

THE BLESSING OF VICTORY FOR GOD'S PEOPLE

14 At that time Amraphel king of Shinar, Arioch king of Ellasar, Kedorlaomer king of Elam, and Tidal king of nations ² went to war against Bera king of Sodom, Birsha king of Gomorrah, Shinab king of Admah, Shemeber king of Zeboyim, and the king of Bela (that is, Zoar). ³ These last five kings joined forces in the Valley of Siddim (that is, the Salt Sea). ⁴ For twelve years they had served Kedorlaomer, but in the thirteenth year they rebelled. ⁵ In the fourteenth year, Kedorlaomer and the kings who were his allies came and defeated the Rephaites in Ashteroth Karnaim, the Zuzites in Ham, the Emites in Shaveh Kiriathaim, ⁶ and the Horites in their hill country of Seir, as far as El Paran, which is near the desert. ⁷ Then they attacked En Mishpat (that is, Kadesh) again, and they conquered all the territory of the Amalekites, as well as the Amorites who were living in Hazezon Tamar.

CONTEMPLATE

Genesis 13:14–18

READ. Read the passage both silently and aloud, listening for the Spirit to speak. Consider the promise in verse 16 and Abram's reaction to the promise in verse 18. Repeat phrases or verses that move you.

MEDITATE. God's promise has implications far beyond Abram and his immediate descendants. What promise do the phrases or verses hold for you? How do you respond when God gives you a promise (v. 18)? What thoughts or emotions do these verses stir?

PRAY. Offer your stirrings to the Lord. He already knows your thoughts, feelings, and convictions. Honestly pray and worship in the confidence that He hears you.

CONTEMPLATE. Commit your day to the Lord, and move forward knowing that all God's promises are "Yes" and "Amen" in Christ Jesus (2 Cor 1:20).

⁸ Then the king of Sodom, the king of Gomorrah, the king of Admah, the king of Zeboyim, and the king of Bela (that is, Zoar) went out and prepared for battle. In the Valley of Siddim they met ⁹ Kedorlaomer king of Elam, Tidal king of nations, Amraphel king of Shinar, and Arioch king of Ellasar. Four kings fought against five. ¹⁰ Now the Valley of Siddim was full of tar pits. When the kings of Sodom and Gomorrah fled, they fell into them, but some survivors fled to the hills. ¹¹ The four victorious kings took all the possessions and food of Sodom and Gomorrah and left. ¹² They also took Abram's nephew Lot and his possessions when they left, for Lot was living in Sodom.

¹³ A fugitive came and told Abram the Hebrew. Now Abram was living by the oaks of Mamre the Amorite, the brother of Eshcol and Aner. (All these were allied by treaty with Abram.) ¹⁴ When Abram heard that his nephew had been taken captive, he mobilized his 318 trained men who had been born in his household, and he pursued the invaders as far as Dan. ¹⁵ Then, during the night, Abram divided his forces against them and defeated them. He chased them as far as Hobah, which is north of Damascus. ¹⁶ He retrieved all the stolen property. He also brought back his nephew Lot and his possessions, as well as the women and the rest of the people.

¹⁷ After Abram returned from defeating Kedorlaomer and the kings who were with him, the king of Sodom went out to meet Abram in the Valley of Shaveh (known as the King's Valley). ¹⁸ Melchizedek king of Salem brought out bread and wine. (Now he was the priest of the Most High God.) ¹⁹ He blessed Abram, saying,

"Blessed be Abram by the Most High God,
Creator of heaven and earth.
20 Worthy of praise is the Most High God,
who delivered your enemies into your hand."

Abram gave Melchizedek a tenth of everything.

²¹ Then the king of Sodom said to Abram, "Give me the people and take the possessions for yourself." ²² But Abram replied to the king of Sodom, "I raise my hand to the LORD, the

JOURNAL

Genesis 14:18–24

REFLECT AND WRITE.

- Why would Abram take nothing from the king of Sodom (see vv. 22–24)? How could you apply Abram's example to your life?

- How does this passage guide you toward a deeper relationship with the Lord?

- What characteristics of God are emphasized in this passage? How should this passage lead you to respond to God?

Most High God, Creator of heaven and earth, and vow ²³ that I will take nothing belonging to you, not even a thread or the strap of a sandal. That way you can never say, 'It is I who made Abram rich.' ²⁴ I will take nothing except compensation for what the young men have eaten. As for the share of the men who went with me—Aner, Eshcol, and Mamre—let them take their share."

THE CUTTING OF THE COVENANT

15 After these things the LORD's message came to Abram in a vision: "Fear not, Abram! I am your shield and the one who will reward you in great abundance."

²But Abram said, "O Sovereign LORD, what will you give me since I continue to be childless, and my heir is Eliezer of Damascus?" ³Abram added, "Since you have not given me a descendant, then look, one born in my house will be my heir!"

⁴But look, the LORD's message came to him: "This man will not be your heir, but instead a son who comes from your own body will be your heir." ⁵The LORD took him outside and said, "Gaze into the sky and count the stars—if you are able to count them!" Then he said to him, "So will your descendants be."

⁶Abram believed the LORD, and the LORD credited it as righteousness to him.

⁷The LORD said to him, "I am the LORD who brought you out from Ur of the Chaldeans to give you this land to possess." ⁸But Abram said, "O Sovereign LORD, by what can I know that I am to possess it?"

⁹The LORD said to him, "Take for me a heifer, a goat, and a ram, each three years old, along with a dove and a young pigeon." ¹⁰So Abram took all these for him and then cut them in two and placed each half opposite the other, but he did not cut the birds in half. ¹¹When birds of prey came down on the carcasses, Abram drove them away.

¹²When the sun went down, Abram fell sound asleep, and great terror overwhelmed him. ¹³Then the LORD said to Abram, "Know for certain that your descendants will be strangers in a foreign country. They will be enslaved and

 CONTEMPLATE

Genesis 15:1–6

READ. Read the passage slowly and look for a phrase that speaks to you. Maybe it's the word of the Lord to Abram (v. 1) or Abram's faith in God (v. 6).

MEDITATE. Repeat the phrase and meditate on it. Would your family and friends characterize you as a person who believes God? What steps can you take to believe Him more? How is God "your shield" and "the one who will reward you in great abundance" (v. 1)?

PRAY. Turn your thoughts to prayer. Ask the Lord to help your unbelief (Mark 9:24) as you continue to abide in Him.

CONTEMPLATE. Abram is counted among our heroes because of his faith and obedience to what God called him to do (Heb 11:8–12). Commit to be a doer of the Word rather than just a hearer (Jas 1:22).

oppressed for 400 years. ¹⁴ But I will execute judgment on the nation that they will serve. Afterward they will come out with many possessions. ¹⁵ But as for you, you will go to your ancestors in peace and be buried at a good old age. ¹⁶ In the fourth generation your descendants will return here, for the sin of the Amorites has not yet reached its limit."

¹⁷ When the sun had gone down and it was dark, a smoking firepot with a flaming torch passed between the animal parts. ¹⁸ That day the LORD made a covenant with Abram: "To your descendants I give this land, from the river of Egypt to the great river, the Euphrates River—¹⁹ the land of the Kenites, Kenizzites, Kadmonites, ²⁰ Hittites, Perizzites, Rephaites, ²¹ Amorites, Canaanites, Girgashites, and Jebusites."

THE BIRTH OF ISHMAEL

16 Now Sarai, Abram's wife, had not given birth to any children, but she had an Egyptian servant named Hagar. ² So Sarai said to Abram, "Since the LORD has prevented me from having children, please sleep with my servant. Perhaps I can have a family by her." Abram did what Sarai told him.

³ So after Abram had lived in Canaan for ten years, Sarai, Abram's wife, gave Hagar, her Egyptian servant, to her husband to be his wife. ⁴ He slept with Hagar, and she became pregnant. Once Hagar realized she was pregnant, she despised Sarai. ⁵ Then Sarai said to Abram, "You have brought this wrong on me! I gave my servant into your embrace, but when she realized that she was pregnant, she despised me. May the LORD judge between you and me!"

⁶ Abram said to Sarai, "Since your servant is under your authority, do to her whatever you think best." Then Sarai treated Hagar harshly, so she ran away from Sarai.

⁷ The angel of the LORD found Hagar near a spring of water in the wilderness—the spring that is along the road to Shur. ⁸ He said, "Hagar, servant of Sarai, where have you come from, and where are you going?" She replied, "I'm running away from my mistress, Sarai."

PICTURE IT

Genesis 15:7–21

PICTURE. Imagine being Abram. What doubts fill your mind? Do you really think God will help you take possession of the land He has promised? Imagine the smells and sights of the animals laid out and arranged. Feel yourself falling into a deep sleep in God's presence and hearing verses 13–16 proclaimed over you. How do these promises make you feel? In a typical covenant, animals would have been split and both parties would have walked between them to say metaphorically, *If I break this covenant, may what happened to these animals happen to me.* What passes between the animals in this covenant (v. 17)? Picture it. What does this represent?

PRAY. Praise God for His unconditional covenant and blessing given to Abram and passed down to you today.

JOURNAL

Genesis 16:1–6

REFLECT AND WRITE.

- What attitudes or feelings do you have as you read this passage?

- How was Sarai justified in her feelings and actions? How was she unjustified?

- What questions come to mind as you read this passage? Write them here, and then ask for God's guidance as you seek answers in His Word.

⁹Then the angel of the LORD said to her, "Return to your mistress and submit to her authority. ¹⁰I will greatly multiply your descendants," the angel of the LORD added, "so that they will be too numerous to count." ¹¹Then the angel of the LORD said to her,

"You are now pregnant
and are about to give birth to a son.
You are to name him Ishmael,
for the LORD has heard your painful groans.
¹² He will be a wild donkey of a man.
He will be hostile to everyone,
and everyone will be hostile to him.
He will live away from his brothers."

¹³So Hagar named the LORD who spoke to her, "You are the God who sees me," for she said, "Here I have seen one who sees me!" ¹⁴That is why the well was called Beer Lahai Roi. (It is located between Kadesh and Bered.)

¹⁵So Hagar gave birth to Abram's son, whom Abram named Ishmael. ¹⁶(Now Abram was 86 years old when Hagar gave birth to Ishmael.)

THE SIGN OF THE COVENANT

17 When Abram was 99 years old, the LORD appeared to him and said, "I am the Sovereign God. Walk before me and be blameless. ²Then I will confirm my covenant between me and you, and I will give you a multitude of descendants."

³Abram bowed down with his face to the ground, and God said to him, ⁴"As for me, this is my covenant with you: You will be the father of a multitude of nations. ⁵No longer will your name be Abram. Instead, your name will be Abraham because I will make you the father of a multitude of nations. ⁶I will make you extremely fruitful. I will make nations of you, and kings will descend from you. ⁷I will confirm my covenant as a perpetual covenant between me and you. It will extend to your descendants after you throughout their generations. I will be your God and the God of your descendants after you. ⁸I will give the whole land of Canaan—the land where you are now residing—to you and your descendants after you as a permanent possession. I will be their God."

PRAYING SCRIPTURE

Genesis 16:11–16

This passage shows God's personal attention to Hagar after she endured a time of hardship. Hagar was Sarai's maidservant. When Sarai could not have a baby, she gave Hagar to her husband, Abram, so Hagar could bear a child for him. But after Hagar became pregnant, Sarai grew jealous and began to mistreat Hagar.

    As you read this passage, pray the words of Genesis 16:13. How has God seen you during your life? Make a brief list; then thank God for His nearness and attention to your needs.

JOURNAL

Genesis 17:1–14

REFLECT AND WRITE.

- Why did God command Abram to walk before Him and be blameless? Why should you do this?

- Why did God change Abram's name? What does God call you, as a member of His family? List as many names, characteristics, and titles as you can.

- Read Romans 2:25–29. How do these verses relate to the original covenant of circumcision in Genesis 17:9–14?

⁹ Then God said to Abraham, "As for you, you must keep the covenantal requirement I am imposing on you and your descendants after you throughout their generations. ¹⁰ This is my requirement that you and your descendants after you must keep: Every male among you must be circumcised. ¹¹ You must circumcise the flesh of your foreskins. This will be a reminder of the covenant between me and you. ¹² Throughout your generations every male among you who is eight days old must be circumcised, whether born in your house or bought with money from any foreigner who is not one of your descendants. ¹³ They must indeed be circumcised, whether born in your house or bought with money. The sign of my covenant will be visible in your flesh as a permanent reminder. ¹⁴ Any uncircumcised male who has not been circumcised in the flesh of his foreskin will be cut off from his people—he has failed to carry out my requirement."

¹⁵ Then God said to Abraham, "As for your wife, you must no longer call her Sarai; Sarah will be her name. ¹⁶ I will bless her and will give you a son through her. I will bless her and she will become a mother of nations. Kings of countries will come from her!"

¹⁷ Then Abraham bowed down with his face to the ground and laughed as he said to himself, "Can a son be born to a man who is a hundred years old? Can Sarah bear a child at the age of ninety?" ¹⁸ Abraham said to God, "O that Ishmael might live before you!"

¹⁹ God said, "No, Sarah your wife is going to bear you a son, and you will name him Isaac. I will confirm my covenant with him as a perpetual covenant for his descendants after him. ²⁰ As for Ishmael, I have heard you. I will indeed bless him, make him fruitful, and give him a multitude of descendants. He will become the father of twelve princes; I will make him into a great nation. ²¹ But I will establish my covenant with Isaac, whom Sarah will bear to you at this set time next year." ²² When he finished speaking with Abraham, God went up from him.

²³ Abraham took his son Ishmael and every male in his household (whether born in his house or bought with money)

CONTEMPLATE

Genesis 17:15–22

READ. Read the passage twice. Enjoy the richness of God and Abraham's dialogue your first time through. Then read it again and choose a phrase to meditate on: "Sarah your wife is going to bear you a son" (v. 19), "Abraham . . . laughed" (v. 17), or "I will establish my covenant with Isaac" (v. 21). Repeat the phrase as you meditate on its meaning and context.

MEDITATE. How can this phrase strengthen your faith?

PRAY. What came to mind as you meditated? Take this to God in prayer. Do you long for something that seems impossible? Boldly submit it to the Father, believing that "nothing will be impossible with God" (Luke 1:37).

CONTEMPLATE. Abide in the shelter of the Almighty, walking by faith and trusting in the Son of God (2 Cor 5:7).

and circumcised them on that very same day, just as God had told him to do. 24 Now Abraham was 99 years old when he was circumcised; 25 his son Ishmael was thirteen years old when he was circumcised. 26 Abraham and his son Ishmael were circumcised on the very same day. 27 All the men of his household, whether born in his household or bought with money from a foreigner, were circumcised with him.

THREE SPECIAL VISITORS

18 The LORD appeared to Abraham by the oaks of Mamre while he was sitting at the entrance to his tent during the hottest time of the day. 2 Abraham looked up and saw three men standing across from him. When he saw them he ran from the entrance of the tent to meet them and bowed low to the ground.

3 He said, "My lord, if I have found favor in your sight, do not pass by and leave your servant. 4 Let a little water be brought so that you may all wash your feet and rest under the tree. 5 And let me get a bit of food so that you may refresh yourselves since you have passed by your servant's home. After that you may be on your way." "All right," they replied, "you may do as you say."

6 So Abraham hurried into the tent and said to Sarah, "Quick! Take three measures of fine flour, knead it, and make bread." 7 Then Abraham ran to the herd and chose a fine, tender calf, and gave it to a servant, who quickly prepared it. 8 Abraham then took some curds and milk, along with the calf that had been prepared, and placed the food before them. They ate while he was standing near them under a tree.

9 Then they asked him, "Where is Sarah your wife?" He replied, "There, in the tent." 10 One of them said, "I will surely return to you when the season comes round again, and your wife Sarah will have a son!" (Now Sarah was listening at the entrance to the tent, not far behind him. 11 Abraham and Sarah were old and advancing in years; Sarah had long since passed menopause.) 12 So Sarah laughed to herself, thinking, "After I am worn out will I have pleasure, especially when my husband is old too?"

JOURNAL

Genesis 18:9–15

REFLECT AND WRITE.

- If you had been Abraham or Sarah, what questions and feelings might you have had about God's news (see v. 10)?

- What is wrong with questioning or doubting God's promises?

- How does verse 10 relate to the virgin birth of Christ (see Isa 7:14; Luke 1:26–38)?

¹³ The LORD said to Abraham, "Why did Sarah laugh and say, 'Will I really have a child when I am old?' ¹⁴ Is anything impossible for the LORD? I will return to you when the season comes round again and Sarah will have a son." ¹⁵ Then Sarah lied, saying, "I did not laugh," because she was afraid. But the LORD said, "No! You did laugh."

ABRAHAM PLEADS FOR SODOM

¹⁶ When the men got up to leave, they looked out over Sodom. (Now Abraham was walking with them to see them on their way.) ¹⁷ Then the LORD said, "Should I hide from Abraham what I am about to do? ¹⁸ After all, Abraham will surely become a great and powerful nation, and all the nations on the earth may receive blessing through him. ¹⁹ I have chosen him so that he may command his children and his household after him to keep the way of the LORD by doing what is right and just. Then the LORD will give to Abraham what he promised him."

²⁰ So the LORD said, "The outcry against Sodom and Gomorrah is so great and their sin so blatant ²¹ that I must go down and see if they are as wicked as the outcry suggests. If not, I want to know."

²² The two men turned and headed toward Sodom, but Abraham was still standing before the LORD. ²³ Abraham approached and said, "Will you really sweep away the godly along with the wicked? ²⁴ What if there are fifty godly people in the city? Will you really wipe it out and not spare the place for the sake of the fifty godly people who are in it? ²⁵ Far be it from you to do such a thing—to kill the godly with the wicked, treating the godly and the wicked alike! Far be it from you! Will not the judge of the whole earth do what is right?"

²⁶ So the LORD replied, "If I find in the city of Sodom fifty godly people, I will spare the whole place for their sake."

²⁷ Then Abraham asked, "Since I have undertaken to speak to the Lord (although I am but dust and ashes), ²⁸ what if there are five less than the fifty godly people? Will you destroy the whole city because five are lacking?" He replied, "I will not destroy it if I find forty-five there."

PRAYING SCRIPTURE

Genesis 18:20–33

As God was about to judge Sodom and Gomorrah, Abraham asked God if He would also destroy the righteous (vv. 23, 25, 28). God made it clear that He would be just and fair, that He would protect the righteous. Pray that God would help people overcome sin in your city (such as violence, abuse, unscrupulous leadership, and godlessness). Also ask God to protect His people as they work to make your city a safer place. Finally, ask God to show you practical ways to take Jesus to people who need Him in your area. For more on God's heart for sinners, read 2 Peter 3:9.

²⁹ Abraham spoke to him again, "What if forty are found there?" He replied, "I will not do it for the sake of the forty."

³⁰ Then Abraham said, "May the Lord not be angry so that I may speak! What if thirty are found there?" He replied, "I will not do it if I find thirty there."

³¹ Abraham said, "Since I have undertaken to speak to the Lord, what if only twenty are found there?" He replied, "I will not destroy it for the sake of the twenty."

³² Finally Abraham said, "May the Lord not be angry so that I may speak just once more. What if ten are found there?" He replied, "I will not destroy it for the sake of the ten."

³³ The LORD went on his way when he had finished speaking to Abraham. Then Abraham returned home.

THE DESTRUCTION OF SODOM AND GOMORRAH

19 The two angels came to Sodom in the evening while Lot was sitting in the city's gateway. When Lot saw them, he got up to meet them and bowed down with his face toward the ground.

² He said, "Here, my lords, please turn aside to your servant's house. Stay the night and wash your feet. Then you can be on your way early in the morning." "No," they replied, "we'll spend the night in the town square."

³ But he urged them persistently, so they turned aside with him and entered his house. He prepared a feast for them, including bread baked without yeast, and they ate. ⁴ Before they could lie down to sleep, all the men—both young and old, from every part of the city of Sodom—surrounded the house. ⁵ They shouted to Lot, "Where are the men who came to you tonight? Bring them out to us so we can take carnal knowledge of them!"

⁶ Lot went outside to them, shutting the door behind him. ⁷ He said, "No, my brothers! Don't act so wickedly! ⁸ Look, I have two daughters who have never been intimate with a man. Let me bring them out to you, and you can do to them whatever you please. Only don't do anything to these men, for they have come under the protection of my roof."

⁹"Out of our way!" they cried, "This man came to live here as a foreigner, and now he dares to judge us! We'll do more harm to you than to them!" They kept pressing in on Lot until they were close enough to break down the door.

¹⁰ So the men inside reached out and pulled Lot back into the house as they shut the door. ¹¹ Then they struck the men who were at the door of the house, from the youngest to the oldest, with blindness. The men outside wore themselves out trying to find the door. ¹² Then the two visitors said to Lot, "Who else do you have here? Do you have any sons-in-law, sons, daughters, or other relatives in the city? Get them out of this place ¹³ because we are about to destroy it. The outcry against this place is so great before the LORD that he has sent us to destroy it."

¹⁴ Then Lot went out and spoke to his sons-in-law who were going to marry his daughters. He said, "Quick, get out of this place because the LORD is about to destroy the city!" But his sons-in-law thought he was ridiculing them.

¹⁵ At dawn the angels hurried Lot along, saying, "Get going! Take your wife and your two daughters who are here, or else you will be destroyed when the city is judged!" ¹⁶ When Lot hesitated, the men grabbed his hand and the hands of his wife and two daughters because the LORD had compassion on them. They led them away and placed them outside the city. ¹⁷ When they had brought them outside, they said, "Run for your lives! Don't look behind you or stop anywhere in the valley! Escape to the mountains or you will be destroyed!"

¹⁸ But Lot said to them, "No, please, Lord! ¹⁹ Your servant has found favor with you, and you have shown me great kindness by sparing my life. But I am not able to escape to the mountains because this disaster will overtake me and I'll die. ²⁰ Look, this town over here is close enough to escape to, and it's just a little one. Let me go there. It's just a little place, isn't it? Then I'll survive."

²¹ "Very well," he replied, "I will grant this request too and will not overthrow the town you mentioned. ²² Run there quickly, for I cannot do anything until you arrive there." (This incident explains why the town was called Zoar.)

CONTEMPLATE

Genesis 19:12–17

READ. Read through this dramatic narrative. Choose a phrase to meditate on. Repeat the phrase as you meditate on its meaning and context.

MEDITATE. How does the phrase reveal God's character? How does it encourage you to pursue a steadfast relationship with Christ?

PRAY. Pray that you will be quick to heed God's warnings in your life with no looking back.

CONTEMPLATE. Take a breath. Remember Christ's finished work on the cross. Submit to the power of the Holy Spirit, who enables you to resist temptation.

 PICTURE IT

Genesis 19:18–29

PICTURE. Place yourself in the scene. Entire cities are about to get wiped off the map because of sin, and you're fleeing the city you once called home, knowing it will be destroyed. How do you feel? Spend a few seconds taking in the scenery. Picture the raining of sulfur. Imagine the smell, the sight, the sounds, and the feel of the air as smoke billows. What thoughts fill your mind? Imagine realizing, after running for a while, that your spouse is no longer with you, but you can't look back to discern his or her fate. How do you feel?

PRAY. Jesus reminded us to "remember Lot's wife!" (Luke 17:32). Pray that you will remember what happens when you take your eyes off Jesus. Pray for confidence in the Lord.

²³ The sun had just risen over the land as Lot reached Zoar. ²⁴ Then the LORD rained down sulfur and fire on Sodom and Gomorrah. It was sent down from the sky by the LORD. ²⁵ So he overthrew those cities and all that region, including all the inhabitants of the cities and the vegetation that grew from the ground. ²⁶ But Lot's wife looked back longingly and was turned into a pillar of salt.

²⁷ Abraham got up early in the morning and went to the place where he had stood before the LORD. ²⁸ He looked out toward Sodom and Gomorrah and all the land of that region. As he did so, he saw the smoke rising up from the land like smoke from a furnace.

²⁹ So when God destroyed the cities of the region, God honored Abraham's request. He removed Lot from the midst of the destruction when he destroyed the cities Lot had lived in.

³⁰ Lot went up from Zoar with his two daughters and settled in the mountains because he was afraid to live in Zoar. So he lived in a cave with his two daughters. ³¹ Later the older daughter said to the younger, "Our father is old, and there is no man in the country to sleep with us, the way everyone does. ³² Come, let's make our father drunk with wine so we can go to bed with him and preserve our family line through our father."

³³ So that night they made their father drunk with wine, and the older daughter came in and went to bed with her father. But he was not aware of when she lay down with him or when she got up. ³⁴ So in the morning the older daughter said to the younger, "Since I went to bed with my father last night, let's make him drunk again tonight. Then you go in and go to bed with him so we can preserve our family line through our father." ³⁵ So they made their father drunk that night as well, and the younger one came and went to bed with him. But he was not aware of when she lay down with him or when she got up.

³⁶ In this way both of Lot's daughters became pregnant by their father. ³⁷ The older daughter gave birth to a son and named him Moab. He is the ancestor of the Moabites of today. ³⁸ The younger daughter also gave birth to a son and named him Ben Ammi. He is the ancestor of the Ammonites of today.

ABRAHAM AND ABIMELECH

20 Abraham journeyed from there to the Negev region and settled between Kadesh and Shur. While he lived as a temporary resident in Gerar, ² Abraham said about his wife Sarah, "She is my sister." So Abimelech, king of Gerar, sent for Sarah and took her.

³ But God appeared to Abimelech in a dream at night and said to him, "You are as good as dead because of the woman you have taken, for she is someone else's wife."

⁴ Now Abimelech had not gone near her. He said, "Lord, would you really slaughter an innocent nation? ⁵ Did Abraham not say to me, 'She is my sister'? And she herself said, 'He is my brother.' I have done this with a clear conscience and with innocent hands!"

⁶ Then in the dream God replied to him, "Yes, I know that you have done this with a clear conscience. That is why I have kept you from sinning against me and why I did not allow you to touch her. ⁷ But now give back the man's wife. Indeed he is a prophet and he will pray for you; thus you will live. But if you don't give her back, know that you will surely die along with all who belong to you."

⁸ Early in the morning Abimelech summoned all his servants. When he told them about all these things, they were terrified. ⁹ Abimelech summoned Abraham and said to him, "What have you done to us? What sin did I commit against you that would cause you to bring such great guilt on me and my kingdom? You have done things to me that should not be done!" ¹⁰ Then Abimelech asked Abraham, "What prompted you to do this thing?"

¹¹ Abraham replied, "Because I thought, 'Surely no one fears God in this place. They will kill me because of my wife.' ¹² What's more, she is indeed my sister, my father's daughter, but not my mother's daughter. She became my wife. ¹³ When God made me wander from my father's house, I told her, 'This is what you can do to show your loyalty to me: Every place we go, say about me, "He is my brother."'"

¹⁴ So Abimelech gave sheep, cattle, and male and female servants to Abraham. He also gave his wife Sarah back to him. ¹⁵ Then Abimelech said, "Look, my land is before you; live wherever you please."

CONTEMPLATE

Genesis 20:1–13

READ. Before you read, ask God to open your mind to His Word. Consider Abraham's behavior in light of his circumstances. Consider Abimelech's response to God in his dream (vv. 4–5) or Abraham's explanation of his actions (vv. 11–13).

MEDITATE. How do you demonstrate a healthy fear of God in your own faith journey? Have you ever withheld the full truth on a matter to protect yourself because of an apparent lack of fear of the Lord in someone else? What was the outcome?

PRAY. Pray that God would help you rightly revere His name. Pray for discernment with unbelievers who hold authority over you and do not have the things of God in mind. Pray for them by name, that they may know the Lord.

CONTEMPLATE. Rest in gratitude that you possess the fear of the Lord.

¹⁶ To Sarah he said, "Look, I have given 1,000 pieces of silver to your 'brother.' This is compensation for you so that you will stand vindicated before all who are with you."

¹⁷ Abraham prayed to God, and God healed Abimelech, as well as his wife and female slaves so that they were able to have children. ¹⁸ For the LORD had caused infertility to strike every woman in the household of Abimelech because he took Sarah, Abraham's wife.

THE BIRTH OF ISAAC

21 The LORD visited Sarah just as he had said he would and did for Sarah what he had promised. ² So Sarah became pregnant and bore Abraham a son in his old age at the appointed time that God had told him. ³ Abraham named his son—whom Sarah bore to him—Isaac. ⁴ When his son Isaac was eight days old, Abraham circumcised him just as God had commanded him to do. ⁵ (Now Abraham was 100 years old when his son Isaac was born to him.)

⁶ Sarah said, "God has made me laugh. Everyone who hears about this will laugh with me." ⁷ She went on to say, "Who would have said to Abraham that Sarah would nurse children? Yet I have given birth to a son for him in his old age!"

⁸ The child grew and was weaned. Abraham prepared a great feast on the day that Isaac was weaned. ⁹ But Sarah noticed the son of Hagar the Egyptian—the son whom Hagar had borne to Abraham—mocking. ¹⁰ So she said to Abraham, "Banish that slave woman and her son, for the son of that slave woman will not be an heir along with my son Isaac!"

¹¹ Sarah's demand displeased Abraham greatly because Ishmael was his son. ¹² But God said to Abraham, "Do not be upset about the boy or your slave wife. Do all that Sarah is telling you because through Isaac your descendants will be counted. ¹³ But I will also make the son of the slave wife into a great nation, for he is your descendant too."

¹⁴ Early in the morning Abraham took some food and a skin of water and gave them to Hagar. He put them on her shoulders, gave her the child, and sent her away. So she went wandering aimlessly through the wilderness of Beer Sheba.

JOURNAL

Genesis 21:1–7

REFLECT AND WRITE.

- How did the Lord fulfill His promise to Sarah and Abraham? What promises has God fulfilled to you?

- Sarah laughed and rejoiced when God fulfilled His promise. How have you experienced joy when God did something greater than you imagined?

CONTEMPLATE

Genesis 21:14–21

READ. Read the passage twice. Then choose a phrase to meditate on. Consider "God heard the boy's voice" or "Don't be afraid, for God has heard" (v. 17). Repeat it silently to yourself.

MEDITATE. How do you connect with these words? What do they reveal about the character of God? How can this phrase lead you to a deeper faith in Christ?

PRAY. Thank God that He hears you and has given you a Spirit not of fear but of power and of love and of self-control (2 Tim 1:7). Just as Hagar and Ishmael experienced God's tender affection, you also can see the Father's tender heart at work in your life and in the lives of others. Ask Him.

CONTEMPLATE. Recall a time God brought about your deliverance in a specific trial. Take heart that His compassions never fail (Lam 3:22).

¹⁵ When the water in the skin was gone, she shoved the child under one of the shrubs. ¹⁶ Then she went and sat down by herself across from him at quite a distance, about a bowshot, away; for she thought, "I refuse to watch the child die." So she sat across from him and wept uncontrollably.

¹⁷ But God heard the boy's voice. The angel of God called to Hagar from heaven and asked her, "What is the matter, Hagar? Don't be afraid, for God has heard the boy's voice right where he is crying. ¹⁸ Get up! Help the boy up and hold him by the hand, for I will make him into a great nation." ¹⁹ Then God enabled Hagar to see a well of water. She went over and filled the skin with water, and then gave the boy a drink.

²⁰ God was with the boy as he grew. He lived in the wilderness and became an archer. ²¹ He lived in the wilderness of Paran. His mother found a wife for him from the land of Egypt.

²² At that time Abimelech and Phicol, the commander of his army, said to Abraham, "God is with you in all that you do. ²³ Now swear to me right here in God's name that you will not deceive me, my children, or my descendants. Show me, and the land where you are staying, the same loyalty that I have shown you."

²⁴ Abraham said, "I swear to do this." ²⁵ But Abraham lodged a complaint against Abimelech concerning a well that Abimelech's servants had seized. ²⁶ "I do not know who has done this thing," Abimelech replied. "Moreover, you did not tell me. I did not hear about it until today."

²⁷ Abraham took some sheep and cattle and gave them to Abimelech. The two of them made a treaty. ²⁸ Then Abraham set seven ewe lambs apart from the flock by themselves. ²⁹ Abimelech asked Abraham, "What is the meaning of these seven ewe lambs that you have set apart?" ³⁰ He replied, "You must take these seven ewe lambs from my hand as legal proof that I dug this well." ³¹ That is why he named that place Beer Sheba, because the two of them swore an oath there.

³² So they made a treaty at Beer Sheba; then Abimelech and Phicol, the commander of his army, returned to the land of the Philistines. ³³ Abraham planted a tamarisk tree in Beer Sheba. There he worshiped the LORD, the eternal God. ³⁴ So Abraham stayed in the land of the Philistines for quite some time.

PRAYING SCRIPTURE

Genesis 21:22–34

The quality of Abraham's life caused Abimelech, an ancient king in the Philistine region of Gerar (Gen 20:2), to notice God's presence. Abimelech saw that God was with Abraham in everything he did (v. 22). Ask God to develop you into a person of great character, so others might notice the difference God makes in your life.

Even in a dispute (vv. 25–26), Abraham dealt justly with Abimelech. Ask God to help you handle your relationships at home and work with kindness and justice. If you face conflicts, put your trust in the God of yesterday, today, and forever (Heb 13:8).

THE SACRIFICE OF ISAAC

22 Some time after these things God tested Abraham. He said to him, "Abraham!" "Here I am!" Abraham replied. ²God said, "Take your son—your only son, whom you love, Isaac—and go to the land of Moriah! Offer him up there as a burnt offering on one of the mountains which I will indicate to you."

³Early in the morning Abraham got up and saddled his donkey. He took two of his young servants with him, along with his son Isaac. When he had cut the wood for the burnt offering, he started out for the place God had spoken to him about.

⁴On the third day Abraham caught sight of the place in the distance. ⁵So he said to his servants, "You two stay here with the donkey while the boy and I go up there. We will worship and then return to you."

⁶Abraham took the wood for the burnt offering and put it on his son Isaac. Then he took the fire and the knife in his hand, and the two of them walked on together. ⁷Isaac said to his father Abraham, "My father?" "What is it, my son?" he replied. "Here is the fire and the wood," Isaac said, "but where is the lamb for the burnt offering?" ⁸"God will provide for himself the lamb for the burnt offering, my son," Abraham replied. The two of them continued on together.

⁹When they came to the place God had told him about, Abraham built the altar there and arranged the wood on it. Next he tied up his son Isaac and placed him on the altar on top of the wood. ¹⁰Then Abraham reached out his hand, took the knife, and prepared to slaughter his son. ¹¹But the angel of the LORD called to him from heaven, "Abraham! Abraham!" "Here I am!" he answered. ¹²"Do not harm the boy!" the angel said. "Do not do anything to him, for now I know that you fear God because you did not withhold your son, your only son, from me."

¹³Abraham looked up and saw behind him a ram caught in the bushes by its horns. So he went over and got the ram and offered it up as a burnt offering instead of his son. ¹⁴And Abraham called the name of that place "The LORD provides." It is said to this day, "In the mountain of the LORD provision will be made."

JOURNAL

Genesis 22:1–5

REFLECT AND WRITE.

- What did Abraham's response say about his posture toward God (see v. 1)? How can you reflect this posture when God calls you?

- Abraham got started "early in the morning" (v. 3). What characteristic of faith does this display? How can you display similar faith?

- How does verse 2 relate to what God did through Jesus?

PICTURE IT

Genesis 22:6–18

PICTURE. After being called to sacrifice Isaac, Abraham travels three days to Moriah. Imagine yourself along on that journey. Abraham and Isaac have just arrived, and now they are going to go worship. As you follow them, you notice they have fire and wood but no animal to sacrifice. Watch Abraham build an altar. How does Abraham bind Isaac? How does Isaac react? What do you think as Abraham raises a knife over Isaac? Do you react or pretend to look away? When the angel of the Lord calls out Abraham's name and intervenes (vv. 11–12), what does Isaac do? How does Abraham respond? How does God's intervention strengthen your faith in Him and His provision?

PRAY. Ask God for the ability to fully trust Him today.

¹⁵ The angel of the LORD called to Abraham a second time from heaven ¹⁶ and said, "I solemnly swear by my own name, decrees the LORD, that because you have done this and have not withheld your son, your only son, ¹⁷ I will indeed bless you, and I will greatly multiply your descendants so that they will be as countless as the stars in the sky or the grains of sand on the seashore. Your descendants will take possession of the strongholds of their enemies. ¹⁸ Because you have obeyed me, all the nations of the earth will pronounce blessings on one another using the name of your descendants."

¹⁹ Then Abraham returned to his servants, and they set out together for Beer Sheba where Abraham stayed.

²⁰ After these things Abraham was told, "Milcah also has borne children to your brother Nahor—²¹ Uz the firstborn, his brother Buz, Kemuel (the father of Aram), ²² Kesed, Hazo, Pildash, Jidlaph, and Bethuel." ²³ (Now Bethuel became the father of Rebekah.) These were the eight sons Milcah bore to Abraham's brother Nahor. ²⁴ His concubine, whose name was Reumah, also bore him children—Tebah, Gaham, Tahash, and Maacah.

THE DEATH OF SARAH

23 Sarah lived 127 years. ² Then she died in Kiriath Arba (that is, Hebron) in the land of Canaan. Abraham went to mourn for Sarah and to weep for her.

³ Then Abraham got up from mourning his dead wife and said to the sons of Heth, ⁴ "I am a foreign resident, a temporary settler, among you. Grant me ownership of a burial site among you so that I may bury my dead."

⁵ The sons of Heth answered Abraham, ⁶ "Listen, sir, you are a mighty prince among us! You may bury your dead in the choicest of our tombs. None of us will refuse you his tomb to prevent you from burying your dead."

⁷ Abraham got up and bowed down to the local people, the sons of Heth. ⁸ Then he said to them, "If you agree that I may bury my dead, then hear me out. Ask Ephron the son of Zohar ⁹ if he will sell me the cave of Machpelah that belongs to

him; it is at the end of his field. Let him sell it to me publicly for the full price, so that I may own it as a burial site."

10 (Now Ephron was sitting among the sons of Heth.) Ephron the Hittite replied to Abraham in the hearing of the sons of Heth—before all who entered the gate of his city—11 "No, my lord! Hear me out. I sell you both the field and the cave that is in it. In the presence of my people I sell it to you. Bury your dead."

12 Abraham bowed before the local people 13 and said to Ephron in their hearing, "Hear me, if you will. I pay to you the price of the field. Take it from me so that I may bury my dead there."

14 Ephron answered Abraham, saying to him, 15 "Hear me, my lord. The land is worth 400 pieces of silver, but what is that between me and you? So bury your dead."

16 So Abraham agreed to Ephron's price and weighed out for him the price that Ephron had quoted in the hearing of the sons of Heth—400 pieces of silver, according to the standard measurement at the time.

17 So Abraham secured Ephron's field in Machpelah, next to Mamre, including the field, the cave that was in it, and all the trees that were in the field and all around its border, 18 as his property in the presence of the sons of Heth before all who entered the gate of Ephron's city.

19 After this Abraham buried his wife Sarah in the cave in the field of Machpelah next to Mamre (that is, Hebron) in the land of Canaan. 20 So Abraham secured the field and the cave that was in it as a burial site from the sons of Heth.

THE WIFE FOR ISAAC

24 Now Abraham was old, well advanced in years, and the LORD had blessed him in everything. 2 Abraham said to his servant, the senior one in his household who was in charge of everything he had, "Put your hand under my thigh 3 so that I may make you solemnly promise by the LORD, the God of heaven and the God of the earth: You must not acquire a wife for my son from the daughters of the Canaanites,

JOURNAL

Genesis 23:12–20

REFLECT AND WRITE.

- As Abraham politely nego-
  tiated with the people of
  the land, he seemed more
  concerned with the burial
  place than with the price
  of the plot. When have you
  been willing to do whatever
  was needed for your family
  or friends?

- Why did Abraham buy a
  burial plot in Canaan instead of burying Sarah with
  her ancestors? How did
  this prove his commitment
  to God in light of God's
  promise to give his descendants the land of Canaan
  as their possession (see
  Gen 17:8)? How might you
  need to step out in faith as
  Abraham did?

among whom I am living. ⁴You must go instead to my country and to my relatives to find a wife for my son Isaac."

⁵The servant asked him, "What if the woman is not willing to come back with me to this land? Must I then take your son back to the land from which you came?"

⁶"Be careful never to take my son back there!" Abraham told him. ⁷"The LORD, the God of heaven, who took me from my father's house and the land of my relatives, promised me with a solemn oath, 'To your descendants I will give this land.' He will send his angel before you so that you may find a wife for my son from there. ⁸But if the woman is not willing to come back with you, you will be free from this oath of mine. But you must not take my son back there!" ⁹So the servant placed his hand under the thigh of his master Abraham and gave his solemn promise he would carry out his wishes.

¹⁰Then the servant took ten of his master's camels and departed with all kinds of gifts from his master at his disposal. He journeyed to the region of Aram Naharaim and the city of Nahor. ¹¹He made the camels kneel down by the well outside the city. It was evening, the time when the women would go out to draw water. ¹²He prayed, "O LORD, God of my master Abraham, guide me today. Be faithful to my master Abraham. ¹³Here I am, standing by the spring, and the daughters of the people who live in the town are coming out to draw water. ¹⁴I will say to a young woman, 'Please lower your jar so I may drink.' May the one you have chosen for your servant Isaac reply, 'Drink, and I'll give your camels water too.' In this way I will know that you have been faithful to my master."

¹⁵Before he had finished praying, there came Rebekah with her water jug on her shoulder. She was the daughter of Bethuel son of Milcah (Milcah was the wife of Abraham's brother Nahor). ¹⁶Now the young woman was very beautiful. She was a virgin; no man had ever been physically intimate with her. She went down to the spring, filled her jug, and came back up. ¹⁷Abraham's servant ran to meet her and said, "Please give me a sip of water from your jug." ¹⁸"Drink, my lord," she replied, and quickly lowering her jug to her hands, she gave him a drink. ¹⁹When she had done so, she said, "I'll draw water for

Genesis 24:10–27

As you meditate on this passage, put yourself in Abraham's shoes. God had told him to leave his homeland (Gen 12). As a result, he lived among people who didn't share his faith. He hoped to find a wife for his son Isaac, but no women in the region followed God. It seemed like an impossible problem. Abraham called his trustworthy servant to find a woman back in his homeland. The situation required God's help, so the servant prayed (v. 12).

Are you facing an impossible situation? Pray the words of Genesis 24:12, making them applicable to your circumstances. How often do you pray bold prayers like the one the servant prayed? God has the power to answer when called upon. Take a few minutes to pray this way before you start your day.

your camels too, until they have drunk as much as they want."
²⁰ She quickly emptied her jug into the watering trough and ran back to the well to draw more water until she had drawn enough for all his camels. ²¹ Silently the man watched her with interest to determine if the LORD had made his journey successful or not.

²² After the camels had finished drinking, the man took out a gold nose ring weighing a beka and two gold wrist bracelets weighing ten shekels and gave them to her. ²³ "Whose daughter are you?" he asked. "Tell me, is there room in your father's house for us to spend the night?"

²⁴ She said to him, "I am the daughter of Bethuel the son of Milcah, whom Milcah bore to Nahor. ²⁵ We have plenty of straw and feed," she added, "and room for you to spend the night."

²⁶ The man bowed his head and worshiped the LORD, ²⁷ saying, "Praised be the LORD, the God of my master Abraham, who has not abandoned his faithful love for my master! The LORD has led me to the house of my master's relatives!"

²⁸ The young woman ran and told her mother's household all about these things. ²⁹ (Now Rebekah had a brother named Laban.) Laban rushed out to meet the man at the spring. ³⁰ When he saw the bracelets on his sister's wrists and the nose ring and heard his sister Rebekah say, "This is what the man said to me," he went out to meet the man. There he was, standing by the camels near the spring. ³¹ Laban said to him, "Come, you who are blessed by the LORD! Why are you standing out here when I have prepared the house and a place for the camels?"

³² So Abraham's servant went to the house and unloaded the camels. Straw and feed were given to the camels, and water was provided so that he and the men who were with him could wash their feet. ³³ When food was served, he said, "I will not eat until I have said what I want to say." "Tell us," Laban said.

³⁴ "I am the servant of Abraham," he began. ³⁵ "The LORD has richly blessed my master and he has become very wealthy. The LORD has given him sheep and cattle, silver and gold, male and female servants, and camels and donkeys. ³⁶ My master's

CONTEMPLATE

Genesis 24:33–51

READ. Read this passage twice. Which phrase speaks to you the most? Perhaps it's "if you have decided to make my journey successful" (v. 42) or "This is the LORD's doing" (v. 50).

MEDITATE. In what ways has God prospered your journey through life so far? What specific examples can you point to? How can you remain mindful of Him rather than taking credit for the success (John 3:27)? Has God ever ordained your steps as He did for Abraham's servant?

PRAY. Transition your specific recollections to an offering of praise and thanks-giving to God for orchestrating your life for your good and for His glory.

CONTEMPLATE. Hold to the truth that "a person plans his course, but the LORD directs his steps" (Prov 16:9).

wife Sarah bore a son to him when she was old, and my master has given him everything he owns. 37 My master made me swear an oath. He said, 'You must not acquire a wife for my son from the daughters of the Canaanites, among whom I am living, 38 but you must go to the family of my father and to my relatives to find a wife for my son.' 39 But I said to my master, 'What if the woman does not want to go with me?' 40 He answered, 'The LORD, before whom I have walked, will send his angel with you. He will make your journey a success and you will find a wife for my son from among my relatives, from my father's family. 41 You will be free from your oath if you go to my relatives and they will not give her to you. Then you will be free from your oath.' 42 When I came to the spring today, I prayed, 'O LORD, God of my master Abraham, if you have decided to make my journey successful, may events unfold as follows: 43 Here I am, standing by the spring. When the young woman goes out to draw water, I'll say, "Please give me a little water to drink from your jug." 44 Then she will reply to me, "Drink, and I'll draw water for your camels too." May that woman be the one whom the LORD has chosen for my master's son.'

45 "Before I finished praying in my heart, along came Rebekah with her water jug on her shoulder! She went down to the spring and drew water. So I said to her, 'Please give me a drink.' 46 She quickly lowered her jug from her shoulder and said, 'Drink, and I'll give your camels water too.' So I drank, and she also gave the camels water. 47 Then I asked her, 'Whose daughter are you?' She replied, 'The daughter of Bethuel the son of Nahor, whom Milcah bore to Nahor.' I put the ring in her nose and the bracelets on her wrists. 48 Then I bowed down and worshiped the LORD. I praised the LORD, the God of my master Abraham, who had led me on the right path to find the granddaughter of my master's brother for his son. 49 Now, if you will show faithful love to my master, tell me. But if not, tell me as well, so that I may go on my way."

50 Then Laban and Bethuel replied, "This is the LORD's doing. Our wishes are of no concern. 51 Rebekah stands here before you. Take her and go so that she may become the wife of your master's son, just as the LORD has decided."

⁵²When Abraham's servant heard their words, he bowed down to the ground before the LORD. ⁵³Then he brought out gold, silver jewelry, and clothing and gave them to Rebekah. He also gave valuable gifts to her brother and to her mother. ⁵⁴After this, he and the men who were with him ate a meal and stayed there overnight.

When they got up in the morning, he said, "Let me leave now so I can return to my master." ⁵⁵But Rebekah's brother and her mother replied, "Let the girl stay with us a few more days, perhaps ten. Then she can go." ⁵⁶But he said to them, "Don't detain me—the LORD has granted me success on my journey. Let me leave now so I may return to my master." ⁵⁷Then they said, "We'll call the girl and find out what she wants to do." ⁵⁸So they called Rebekah and asked her, "Do you want to go with this man?" She replied, "I want to go."

⁵⁹So they sent their sister Rebekah on her way, accompanied by her female attendant, with Abraham's servant and his men. ⁶⁰They blessed Rebekah with these words:

"Our sister, may you become the mother
    of thousands of ten thousands!
May your descendants possess the
    strongholds of their enemies."

⁶¹Then Rebekah and her female servants mounted the camels and rode away with the man. So Abraham's servant took Rebekah and left.

⁶²Now Isaac came from Beer Lahai Roi, for he was living in the Negev. ⁶³He went out to relax in the field in the early evening. Then he looked up and saw that there were camels approaching. ⁶⁴Rebekah looked up and saw Isaac. She got down from her camel ⁶⁵and asked Abraham's servant, "Who is that man walking in the field toward us?" "That is my master," the servant replied. So she took her veil and covered herself.

⁶⁶The servant told Isaac everything that had happened. ⁶⁷Then Isaac brought Rebekah into his mother Sarah's tent. He took her as his wife and loved her. So Isaac was comforted after his mother's death.

JOURNAL

Genesis 24:59–67

REFLECT AND WRITE.

- How does verse 60 relate to God's promise to Abram (see Gen 12)? Read Galatians 3:26–4:7. How did Christ bring new meaning to God's promise to Abram?

- Death and new life are daily realities in our world. How does Genesis 24:66–67 illustrate this? How can knowing that God is in control encourage you regardless of what you face?

THE DEATH OF ABRAHAM

25 Abraham had taken another wife, named Keturah. ²She bore him Zimran, Jokshan, Medan, Midian, Ishbak, and Shuah. ³Jokshan became the father of Sheba and Dedan. The descendants of Dedan were the Asshurites, Letushites, and Leummites. ⁴The sons of Midian were Ephah, Epher, Hanoch, Abida, and Eldaah. All these were descendants of Keturah.

⁵Everything he owned Abraham left to his son Isaac. ⁶But while he was still alive, Abraham gave gifts to the sons of his concubines and sent them off to the east, away from his son Isaac.

⁷Abraham lived a total of 175 years. ⁸Then Abraham breathed his last and died at a good old age, an old man who had lived a full life. He joined his ancestors. ⁹His sons Isaac and Ishmael buried him in the cave of Machpelah near Mamre, in the field of Ephron the son of Zohar, the Hittite. ¹⁰This was the field Abraham had purchased from the sons of Heth. There Abraham was buried with his wife Sarah. ¹¹After Abraham's death, God blessed his son Isaac. Isaac lived near Beer Lahai Roi.

THE SONS OF ISHMAEL

¹²This is the account of Abraham's son Ishmael, whom Hagar the Egyptian, Sarah's servant, bore to Abraham.

¹³These are the names of Ishmael's sons, by their names according to their records: Nebaioth (Ishmael's firstborn), Kedar, Adbeel, Mibsam, ¹⁴Mishma, Dumah, Massa, ¹⁵Hadad, Tema, Jetur, Naphish, and Kedemah. ¹⁶These are the sons of Ishmael, and these are their names by their settlements and their camps—twelve princes according to their clans.

¹⁷Ishmael lived a total of 137 years. He breathed his last and died; then he joined his ancestors. ¹⁸His descendants settled from Havilah to Shur, which runs next to Egypt all the way to Asshur. They settled away from all their relatives.

JACOB AND ESAU

¹⁹This is the account of Isaac, the son of Abraham.

Abraham became the father of Isaac. ²⁰When Isaac was forty years old, he married Rebekah, the daughter of Bethuel the Aramean from Paddan Aram and sister of Laban the Aramean.

Genesis 25:7–11

This passage serves as a brief obituary for Abraham. He sinned, but he was also a man of faith. His faith is even mentioned in Romans 4 and Hebrews 11:8–12. God used Abraham to make a great nation, one that today has members "like the innumerable grains of sand on the seashore" (Heb 11:12). Do you think God greeted Abraham at his death with the words "Well done, good and faithful slave!" (Matt 25:23)? Pray for this outcome in your life. Pray that God develops your faith and uses you for His purposes.

²¹ Isaac prayed to the LORD on behalf of his wife because she was childless. The LORD answered his prayer, and his wife Rebekah became pregnant. ²² But the children struggled inside her, and she said, "Why is this happening to me?" So she asked the LORD, ²³ and the LORD said to her,

"Two nations are in your womb,
and two peoples will be separated from within you.
One people will be stronger than the other,
and the older will serve the younger."

²⁴ When the time came for Rebekah to give birth, there were twins in her womb. ²⁵ The first came out reddish all over, like a hairy garment, so they named him Esau. ²⁶ When his brother came out with his hand clutching Esau's heel, they named him Jacob. Isaac was sixty years old when they were born.

²⁷ When the boys grew up, Esau became a skilled hunter, a man of the open fields, but Jacob was an even-tempered man, living in tents. ²⁸ Isaac loved Esau because he had a taste for fresh game, but Rebekah loved Jacob.

²⁹ Now Jacob cooked some stew, and when Esau came in from the open fields, he was famished. ³⁰ So Esau said to Jacob, "Feed me some of the red stuff—yes, this red stuff—because I'm starving!" (That is why he was also called Edom.)

³¹ But Jacob replied, "First sell me your birthright." ³² "Look," said Esau, "I'm about to die! What use is the birthright to me?" ³³ But Jacob said, "Swear an oath to me now." So Esau swore an oath to him and sold his birthright to Jacob.

³⁴ Then Jacob gave Esau some bread and lentil stew; Esau ate and drank, then got up and went out. So Esau despised his birthright.

ISAAC AND ABIMELECH

26 There was a famine in the land, subsequent to the earlier famine that occurred in the days of Abraham. Isaac went to Abimelech king of the Philistines at Gerar. ² The LORD appeared to Isaac and said, "Do not go down to Egypt; settle down in the land that I will point out to you. ³ Stay in this land. Then I will be with you and will bless you, for I will give all these

PICTURE IT

Genesis 25:27–34

PICTURE. This passage
unpacks the differences
between Jacob and Esau. Try
to gain a good mental image
of Esau (Gen 25:25). Next
think of Jacob based on the
description of him (v. 27).
Now imagine you're with
them when Esau, a hunter,
comes home after being out
all day and Jacob is cooking.
Picture Esau's hungry and
irritated demeanor as he
enters the house. Is it cruel
for Jacob to ask for Esau's
birthright? What leads Esau
to do as his brother asks?
With what tone does Jacob
speak in verses 31–33? How
do you think Esau feels as he
leaves the table?

PRAY. What does God say
to you through the imagery
of this passage? Thank Him
for making His Word come
alive today.

lands to you and to your descendants, and I will fulfill the solemn promise I made to your father Abraham. 4 I will multiply your descendants so they will be as numerous as the stars in the sky, and I will give them all these lands. All the nations of the earth will pronounce blessings on one another using the name of your descendants. 5 All this will come to pass because Abraham obeyed me and kept my charge, my commandments, my statutes, and my laws." 6 So Isaac settled in Gerar.

7 When the men of that place asked him about his wife, he replied, "She is my sister." He was afraid to say, "She is my wife," for he thought to himself, "The men of this place will kill me to get Rebekah because she is very beautiful."

8 After Isaac had been there a long time, Abimelech king of the Philistines happened to look out a window and observed Isaac caressing his wife Rebekah. 9 So Abimelech summoned Isaac and said, "She is really your wife! Why did you say, 'She is my sister'?" Isaac replied, "Because I thought someone might kill me to get her."

10 Then Abimelech exclaimed, "What in the world have you done to us? One of the men nearly took your wife to bed, and you would have brought guilt on us!" 11 So Abimelech commanded all the people, "Whoever touches this man or his wife will surely be put to death."

12 When Isaac planted in that land, he reaped in the same year a hundred times what he had sown, because the LORD blessed him. 13 The man became wealthy. His influence continued to grow until he became very prominent. 14 He had so many sheep and cattle and such a great household of servants that the Philistines became jealous of him. 15 So the Philistines took dirt and filled up all the wells that his father's servants had dug back in the days of his father Abraham.

16 Then Abimelech said to Isaac, "Leave us and go elsewhere, for you have become much more powerful than we are." 17 So Isaac left there and settled in the Gerar Valley. 18 Isaac reopened the wells that had been dug back in the days of his father Abraham, for the Philistines had stopped them up after Abraham died. Isaac gave these wells the same names his father had given them.

JOURNAL

Genesis 26:6–11

REFLECT AND WRITE.

• How are these verses similar to the story in Genesis 20:1–18? What is different about the two stories?

• Why do you think Isaac was afraid even though he had God's promise? What difficult decisions are you facing? How can God's promises guide you to do the right thing?

¹⁹ When Isaac's servants dug in the valley and discovered a well with fresh flowing water there, ²⁰ the herdsmen of Gerar quarreled with Isaac's herdsmen, saying, "The water belongs to us!" So Isaac named the well Esek because they argued with him about it. ²¹ His servants dug another well, but they quarreled over it too, so Isaac named it Sitnah. ²² Then he moved away from there and dug another well. They did not quarrel over it, so Isaac named it Rehoboth, saying, "For now the LORD has made room for us, and we will prosper in the land."

²³ From there Isaac went up to Beer Sheba. ²⁴ The LORD appeared to him that night and said, "I am the God of your father Abraham. Do not be afraid, for I am with you. I will bless you and multiply your descendants for the sake of my servant Abraham." ²⁵ Then Isaac built an altar there and worshiped the LORD. He pitched his tent there, and his servants dug a well.

²⁶ Now Abimelech had come to him from Gerar along with Ahuzzah his friend and Phicol the commander of his army. ²⁷ Isaac asked them, "Why have you come to me? You hate me and sent me away from you." ²⁸ They replied, "We could plainly see that the LORD is with you. So we decided there should be a pact between us—between us and you. Allow us to make a treaty with you ²⁹ so that you will not do us any harm, just as we have not harmed you, but have always treated you well before sending you away in peace. Now you are blessed by the LORD."

³⁰ So Isaac held a feast for them and they celebrated. ³¹ Early in the morning the men made a treaty with each other. Isaac sent them off; they separated on good terms.

³² That day Isaac's servants came and told him about the well they had dug. "We've found water," they reported. ³³ So he named it Shibah; that is why the name of the city has been Beer Sheba to this day.

³⁴ When Esau was forty years old, he married Judith the daughter of Beeri the Hittite, as well as Basemath the daughter of Elon the Hittite. ³⁵ They caused Isaac and Rebekah great anxiety.

CONTEMPLATE

Genesis 26:23–29

READ. Read the passage slowly. Which word or phrase speaks to you? Consider God's promise to Isaac (v. 24) or Abimelech's peace proposal (vv. 28–29).

MEDITATE. How do you see God's promise to Isaac reflected in Abimelech's peace proposal? How does this faithful account of God upholding His promise to Isaac encourage you to abide in Christ? How does this Scripture passage apply to you?

PRAY. Pray to sense God's nearness in your dealings with family, friends, and those in the wider world. Ask Him to make you aware of His fatherly love. Praise Him for specific blessings He has bestowed on you or your family.

CONTEMPLATE. Rest in the assurance that the God who walked with Abraham and Isaac is the same God who promises to walk with you.

JACOB CHEATS ESAU OUT OF THE BLESSING

27 When Isaac was old and his eyes were so weak that he was almost blind, he called his older son Esau and said to him, "My son!" "Here I am!" Esau replied. ² Isaac said, "Since I am so old, I could die at any time. ³ Therefore, take your weapons—your quiver and your bow—and go out into the open fields and hunt down some wild game for me. ⁴ Then prepare for me some tasty food, the kind I love, and bring it to me. Then I will eat it so that I may bless you before I die."

⁵ Now Rebekah had been listening while Isaac spoke to his son Esau. When Esau went out to the open fields to hunt down some wild game and bring it back, ⁶ Rebekah said to her son Jacob, "Look, I overheard your father tell your brother Esau, ⁷ 'Bring me some wild game and prepare for me some tasty food. Then I will eat it and bless you in the presence of the LORD before I die.' ⁸ Now then, my son, do exactly what I tell you! ⁹ Go to the flock and get me two of the best young goats. I'll prepare them in a tasty way for your father, just the way he loves them. ¹⁰ Then you will take it to your father. Thus he will eat it and bless you before he dies."

¹¹ "But Esau my brother is a hairy man," Jacob protested to his mother Rebekah, "and I have smooth skin! ¹² My father may touch me! Then he'll think I'm mocking him and I'll bring a curse on myself instead of a blessing." ¹³ So his mother told him, "Any curse against you will fall on me, my son! Just obey me! Go and get them for me!"

¹⁴ So he went and got the goats and brought them to his mother. She prepared some tasty food, just the way his father loved it. ¹⁵ Then Rebekah took her older son Esau's best clothes, which she had with her in the house, and put them on her younger son Jacob. ¹⁶ She put the skins of the young goats on his hands and the smooth part of his neck. ¹⁷ Then she handed the tasty food and the bread she had made to her son Jacob.

¹⁸ He went to his father and said, "My father!" Isaac replied, "Here I am. Which are you, my son?" ¹⁹ Jacob said to his father, "I am Esau, your firstborn. I've done as you told me. Now sit up and eat some of my wild game so that you can bless me." ²⁰ But Isaac asked his son, "How in the world did you find it

JOURNAL

Genesis 27:1–29

REFLECT AND WRITE.

- What feelings, thoughts, or questions do you have as you read this story?

- Why would Jacob and his mother want to deceive his father? How does God take this action and use it for His glory and Jacob's good? How have you seen God use something for His glory that was initially intended for hurt or deceit?

_____

_____

_____

_____

_____

_____

_____

_____

_____

_____

_____

_____

_____

_____

_____

_____

_____

_____

_____

_____

_____

_____

so quickly, my son?" "Because the LORD your God brought it to me," he replied. [21] Then Isaac said to Jacob, "Come closer so I can touch you, my son, and know for certain if you really are my son Esau." [22] So Jacob went over to his father Isaac, who felt him and said, "The voice is Jacob's, but the hands are Esau's." [23] He did not recognize him because his hands were hairy, like his brother Esau's hands. So Isaac blessed Jacob. [24] Then he asked, "Are you really my son Esau?" "I am," Jacob replied. [25] Isaac said, "Bring some of the wild game for me to eat, my son. Then I will bless you." So Jacob brought it to him, and he ate it. He also brought him wine, and Isaac drank. [26] Then his father Isaac said to him, "Come here and kiss me, my son." [27] So Jacob went over and kissed him. When Isaac caught the scent of his clothing, he blessed him, saying,

> "Yes, my son smells
> like the scent of an open field
> which the LORD has blessed.

[28]
> May God give you
> the dew of the sky
> and the richness of the earth,
> and plenty of grain and new wine.

[29]
> May peoples serve you
> and nations bow down to you.
> You will be lord over your brothers,
> and the sons of your mother will bow down to you.
> May those who curse you be cursed,
> and those who bless you be blessed."

[30] Isaac had just finished blessing Jacob, and Jacob had scarcely left his father's presence, when his brother Esau returned from the hunt. [31] He also prepared some tasty food and brought it to his father. Esau said to him, "My father, get up and eat some of your son's wild game. Then you can bless me." [32] His father Isaac asked, "Who are you?" "I am your firstborn son," he replied, "Esau!" [33] Isaac began to shake violently and asked, "Then who else hunted game and brought it to me? I ate all of it just before you arrived, and I blessed him. He will indeed be blessed!"

CONTEMPLATE

Genesis 27:30–40

READ. Read the passage and choose a phrase to meditate on. Consider "He will indeed be blessed!" (v. 33) or "Bless me too, my father!" (v. 34).

MEDITATE. How would it feel to be Esau at this moment? How does an account of a father stirring his heart to decree a blessing over his children speak to you? What might apply to you personally inside this passage?

PRAY. Maintain a listening posture. If you feel or have felt hopeless like Esau, ask God to bring you hope and understanding to know His plan for you. Submit that His plan is greater than your own and will ultimately reveal His sovereign glory.

CONTEMPLATE. You have peace with God because of Jesus. You can rejoice in the hope of the promise of God's glory through tribulations; this is a hope that does not disappoint (Rom 5:1–5).

34 When Esau heard his father's words, he wailed loudly and bitterly. He said to his father, "Bless me too, my father!" 35 But Isaac replied, "Your brother came in here deceitfully and took away your blessing." 36 Esau exclaimed, "Jacob is the right name for him! He has tripped me up two times! He took away my birthright, and now, look, he has taken away my blessing!" Then he asked, "Have you not kept back a blessing for me?"

37 Isaac replied to Esau, "Look! I have made him lord over you. I have made all his relatives his servants and provided him with grain and new wine. What is left that I can do for you, my son?" 38 Esau said to his father, "Do you have only that one blessing, my father? Bless me too!" Then Esau wept loudly.

39 So his father Isaac said to him,

"See here, your home will be by the
    richness of the earth,
and by the dew of the sky above.
40   You will live by your sword
but you will serve your brother.
When you grow restless,
you will tear off his yoke
from your neck."

41 So Esau hated Jacob because of the blessing his father had given to his brother. Esau said privately, "The time of mourning for my father is near; then I will kill my brother Jacob!"

42 When Rebekah heard what her older son Esau had said, she quickly summoned her younger son Jacob and told him, "Look, your brother Esau is planning to get revenge by killing you. 43 Now then, my son, do what I say. Run away immediately to my brother Laban in Haran. 44 Live with him for a little while until your brother's rage subsides. 45 Stay there until your brother's anger against you subsides and he forgets what you did to him. Then I'll send someone to bring you back from there. Why should I lose both of you in one day?"

46 Then Rebekah said to Isaac, "I am deeply depressed because of the daughters of Heth. If Jacob were to marry one of these daughters of Heth who live in this land, I would want to die!"

28

So Isaac called for Jacob and blessed him. Then he commanded him, "You must not marry a Canaanite woman! ² Leave immediately for Paddan Aram! Go to the house of Bethuel, your mother's father, and find yourself a wife there, among the daughters of Laban, your mother's brother. ³ May the Sovereign God bless you! May he make you fruitful and give you a multitude of descendants! Then you will become a large nation. ⁴ May he give you and your descendants the blessing he gave to Abraham so that you may possess the land God gave to Abraham, the land where you have been living as a temporary resident." ⁵ So Isaac sent Jacob on his way, and he went to Paddan Aram, to Laban son of Bethuel the Aramean and brother of Rebekah, the mother of Jacob and Esau.

⁶ Esau saw that Isaac had blessed Jacob and sent him off to Paddan Aram to find a wife there. As he blessed him, Isaac commanded him, "You must not marry a Canaanite woman." ⁷ Jacob obeyed his father and mother and left for Paddan Aram. ⁸ Then Esau realized that the Canaanite women were displeasing to his father Isaac. ⁹ So Esau went to Ishmael and married Mahalath, the sister of Nebaioth and daughter of Abraham's son Ishmael, along with the wives he already had.

JACOB'S DREAM AT BETHEL

¹⁰ Meanwhile Jacob left Beer Sheba and set out for Haran. ¹¹ He reached a certain place where he decided to camp because the sun had gone down. He took one of the stones and placed it near his head. Then he fell asleep in that place ¹² and had a dream. He saw a stairway erected on the earth with its top reaching to the heavens. The angels of God were going up and coming down it ¹³ and the LORD stood at its top. He said, "I am the LORD, the God of your grandfather Abraham and the God of your father Isaac. I will give you and your descendants the ground you are lying on. ¹⁴ Your descendants will be like the dust of the earth, and you will spread out to the west, east, north, and south. And so all the families of the earth may receive blessings through you and through your descendants. ¹⁵ I am with you! I will protect you wherever you go and will bring you back to this land. I will not leave you until I have done what I promised you!"

PRAYING SCRIPTURE

Genesis 28:1–4

Who has bestowed a blessing on you, believed in your calling, or inspired you to walk in faith? Take a few minutes to thank God for those people. Then pray Genesis 28:3–4 for your life, making each line personally applicable. He gave you His Son, Jesus, as the way to abundant life in Him. Remember today that God has blessed you more than you can imagine.

Notice also that the blessing was not just for Jacob. Isaac also referred to Jacob's descendants and future generations. Why do you think Isaac had such concern for people in the distant future?

CONTEMPLATE

Genesis 28:13–22

READ. Read the passage twice. Choose a verse to dwell on that speaks to you. Repeat its words until it begins to take root.

MEDITATE. What makes you Abraham's descendant (see Gal 3:29)? How have you seen God "protect you wherever you go" (v. 15)? Consider Jacob's response to the words the Lord spoke over him (vv. 16–22). How can you respond to those words?

PRAY. What emotions or convictions came to the surface? Take them to God in prayer. Pray that God will help you to be mindful that He is with you and will keep you wherever you go.

CONTEMPLATE. Take a few moments to be silent in His presence. Put away the thoughts of the day, and rest in His love and His delight over you (Zeph 3:17).

¹⁶ Then Jacob woke up and thought, "Surely the LORD is in this place, but I did not realize it!" ¹⁷ He was afraid and said, "What an awesome place this is! This is nothing else than the house of God! This is the gate of heaven!"

¹⁸ Early in the morning Jacob took the stone he had placed near his head and set it up as a sacred stone. Then he poured oil on top of it. ¹⁹ He called that place Bethel, although the former name of the town was Luz. ²⁰ Then Jacob made a vow, saying, "If God is with me and protects me on this journey I am taking and gives me food to eat and clothing to wear, ²¹ and I return safely to my father's home, then the LORD will become my God. ²² Then this stone that I have set up as a sacred stone will be the house of God, and I will surely give you back a tenth of everything you give me."

THE MARRIAGES OF JACOB

29 So Jacob moved on and came to the land of the eastern people. ² He saw in the field a well with three flocks of sheep lying beside it, because the flocks were watered from that well. Now a large stone covered the mouth of the well. ³ When all the flocks were gathered there, the shepherds would roll the stone off the mouth of the well and water the sheep. Then they would put the stone back in its place over the well's mouth.

⁴ Jacob asked them, "My brothers, where are you from?" They replied, "We're from Haran." ⁵ So he said to them, "Do you know Laban, the grandson of Nahor?" "We know him," they said. ⁶ "Is he well?" Jacob asked. They replied, "He is well. Now look, here comes his daughter Rachel with the sheep." ⁷ Then Jacob said, "Since it is still the middle of the day, it is not time for the flocks to be gathered. You should water the sheep and then go and let them graze some more." ⁸ "We can't," they said, "until all the flocks are gathered and the stone is rolled off the mouth of the well. Then we water the sheep."

⁹ While he was still speaking with them, Rachel arrived with her father's sheep, for she was tending them. ¹⁰ When Jacob saw Rachel, the daughter of his uncle Laban, and the sheep of his uncle Laban, he went over and rolled the stone off the mouth of the well and watered the sheep of his uncle

Laban. ¹¹Then Jacob kissed Rachel and began to weep loudly. ¹²When Jacob explained to Rachel that he was a relative of her father and the son of Rebekah, she ran and told her father. ¹³When Laban heard this news about Jacob, his sister's son, he rushed out to meet him. He embraced him and kissed him and brought him to his house. Jacob told Laban how he was related to him. ¹⁴Then Laban said to him, "You are indeed my own flesh and blood." So Jacob stayed with him for a month.

¹⁵Then Laban said to Jacob, "Should you work for me for nothing because you are my relative? Tell me what your wages should be." ¹⁶(Now Laban had two daughters; the older one was named Leah, and the younger one Rachel. ¹⁷Leah's eyes were tender, but Rachel had a lovely figure and beautiful appearance.) ¹⁸Since Jacob had fallen in love with Rachel, he said, "I'll serve you seven years in exchange for your younger daughter Rachel." ¹⁹Laban replied, "I'd rather give her to you than to another man. Stay with me." ²⁰So Jacob worked for seven years to acquire Rachel. But they seemed like only a few days to him because his love for her was so great.

²¹Finally Jacob said to Laban, "Give me my wife, for my time of service is up. And I want to sleep with her." ²²So Laban invited all the people of that place and prepared a feast. ²³In the evening he brought his daughter Leah to Jacob, and he slept with her. ²⁴(Laban gave his female servant Zilpah to his daughter Leah to be her servant.)

²⁵In the morning Jacob discovered it was Leah! So Jacob said to Laban, "What in the world have you done to me? Didn't I work for you in exchange for Rachel? Why have you tricked me?" ²⁶"It is not our custom here," Laban replied, "to give the younger daughter in marriage before the firstborn. ²⁷Complete my older daughter's bridal week. Then we will give you the younger one too, in exchange for seven more years of work."

²⁸Jacob did as Laban said. When Jacob completed Leah's bridal week, Laban gave him his daughter Rachel to be his wife. ²⁹(Laban gave his female servant Bilhah to his daughter Rachel to be her servant.) ³⁰Jacob slept with Rachel as well. He also loved Rachel more than Leah. Then he worked for Laban for seven more years.

PRAYING SCRIPTURE

Genesis 29:18–30

These verses describe one of the great love stories in the Bible. Jacob loved Rachel so much that he was willing to work as a servant for fourteen years to win her hand in marriage. As you read this story, consider today's common approaches to dating and marriage. What can we learn from this story? How does Jacob's love for Rachel give you a glimpse of God's love for you?

Next, focus on Laban's deception. Have you ever been deceived by someone the way Jacob was by Laban? Have you struggled to forgive that person? Ask God to help you let go of your anger.

THE FAMILY OF JACOB

[31] When the LORD saw that Leah was unloved, he enabled her to become pregnant while Rachel remained childless. [32] So Leah became pregnant and gave birth to a son. She named him Reuben, for she said, "The LORD has looked with pity on my oppressed condition. Surely my husband will love me now."

[33] She became pregnant again and had another son. She said, "Because the LORD heard that I was unloved, he gave me this one too." So she named him Simeon.

[34] She became pregnant again and had another son. She said, "Now this time my husband will show me affection, because I have given birth to three sons for him." That is why he was named Levi.

[35] She became pregnant again and had another son. She said, "This time I will praise the LORD." That is why she named him Judah. Then she stopped having children.

30 When Rachel saw that she could not give Jacob children, she became jealous of her sister. She said to Jacob, "Give me children or I'll die!" [2] Jacob became furious with Rachel and exclaimed, "Am I in the place of God, who has kept you from having children?" [3] She replied, "Here is my servant Bilhah! Sleep with her so that she can bear children for me and I can have a family through her."

[4] So Rachel gave him her servant Bilhah as a wife, and Jacob slept with her. [5] Bilhah became pregnant and gave Jacob a son. [6] Then Rachel said, "God has vindicated me. He has responded to my prayer and given me a son." That is why she named him Dan.

[7] Bilhah, Rachel's servant, became pregnant again and gave Jacob another son. [8] Then Rachel said, "I have fought a desperate struggle with my sister, but I have won." So she named him Naphtali.

[9] When Leah saw that she had stopped having children, she gave her servant Zilpah to Jacob as a wife. [10] Soon Leah's servant Zilpah gave Jacob a son. [11] Leah said, "How fortunate!" So she named him Gad.

JOURNAL

Genesis 29:31–35

REFLECT AND WRITE.

• The twelve tribes of Israel came from Jacob's sons. What is significant about Leah's sons and their respective tribes? (See Gen 49 for Jacob's blessings on each of his sons.) How does this heighten her importance in this story?

• How do you relate to Leah's emotions? How has God shown His love and care for you?

¹²Then Leah's servant Zilpah gave Jacob another son. ¹³Leah said, "How happy I am, for women will call me happy!" So she named him Asher.

¹⁴At the time of the wheat harvest Reuben went out and found some mandrake plants in a field and brought them to his mother Leah. Rachel said to Leah, "Give me some of your son's mandrakes." ¹⁵But Leah replied, "Wasn't it enough that you've taken away my husband? Would you take away my son's mandrakes too?" "All right," Rachel said, "he may go to bed with you tonight in exchange for your son's mandrakes." ¹⁶When Jacob came in from the fields that evening, Leah went out to meet him and said, "You must sleep with me because I have paid for your services with my son's mandrakes." So he went to bed with her that night. ¹⁷God paid attention to Leah; she became pregnant and gave Jacob a son for the fifth time. ¹⁸Then Leah said, "God has granted me a reward because I gave my servant to my husband as a wife." So she named him Issachar.

¹⁹Leah became pregnant again and gave Jacob a son for the sixth time. ²⁰Then Leah said, "God has given me a good gift. Now my husband will honor me because I have given him six sons." So she named him Zebulun.

²¹After that she gave birth to a daughter and named her Dinah.

²²Then God took note of Rachel. He paid attention to her and enabled her to become pregnant. ²³She became pregnant and gave birth to a son. Then she said, "God has taken away my shame." ²⁴She named him Joseph, saying, "May the LORD give me yet another son."

THE FLOCKS OF JACOB

²⁵After Rachel had given birth to Joseph, Jacob said to Laban, "Send me on my way so that I can go home to my own country. ²⁶Let me take my wives and my children whom I have acquired by working for you. Then I'll depart, because you know how hard I've worked for you."

²⁷But Laban said to him, "If I have found favor in your sight, please stay here, for I have learned by divination that the LORD has blessed me on account of you." ²⁸He added, "Just name your wages—I'll pay whatever you want."

CONTEMPLATE

Genesis 30:17–24

READ. Read, then reread, the passage. Find a word or phrase to dwell on, and linger with it a moment. Consider "God took note of Rachel" (v. 22) or "God has taken away my shame" (v. 23). Repeat the word or phrase.

MEDITATE. What do you know about Jacob's twelve sons? What do you know about Joseph? As God remembered Rachel, in what way has God remembered you?

PRAY. Thank God for the family records in Scripture. Thank Him that He has revealed the lineage of Jesus through the line of Jacob. Praise Him for the details of Himself and His Son that He has chosen to provide.

CONTEMPLATE. You also are remembered by God, who cares for you and hears you when you pray. Take a moment to linger in His presence.

²⁹ "You know how I have worked for you," Jacob replied, "and how well your livestock have fared under my care. ³⁰ Indeed, you had little before I arrived, but now your possessions have increased many times over. The LORD has blessed you wherever I worked. But now, how long must it be before I do something for my own family too?"

³¹ So Laban asked, "What should I give you?" "You don't need to give me a thing," Jacob replied, "but if you agree to this one condition, I will continue to care for your flocks and protect them: ³² Let me walk among all your flocks today and remove from them every speckled or spotted sheep, every dark-colored lamb, and the spotted or speckled goats. These animals will be my wages. ³³ My integrity will testify for me later on. When you come to verify that I've taken only the wages we agreed on, if I have in my possession any goat that is not speckled or spotted or any sheep that is not dark-colored, it will be considered stolen." ³⁴ "Agreed!" said Laban, "It will be as you say."

³⁵ So that day Laban removed the male goats that were streaked or spotted, all the female goats that were speckled or spotted (all that had any white on them), and all the dark-colored lambs, and put them in the care of his sons. ³⁶ Then he separated them from Jacob by a three-day journey, while Jacob was taking care of the rest of Laban's flocks.

³⁷ But Jacob took fresh-cut branches from poplar, almond, and plane trees. He made white streaks by peeling them, making the white inner wood in the branches visible. ³⁸ Then he set up the peeled branches in all the watering troughs where the flocks came to drink. He set up the branches in front of the flocks when they were in heat and came to drink. ³⁹ When the sheep mated in front of the branches, they gave birth to young that were streaked or speckled or spotted. ⁴⁰ Jacob removed these lambs, but he made the rest of the flock face the streaked and completely dark-colored animals in Laban's flock. So he made separate flocks for himself and did not mix them with Laban's flocks. ⁴¹ When the stronger females were in heat, Jacob would set up the branches in the troughs in front of the flock, so they would mate near the branches. ⁴² But if the animals were weaker, he did not set the branches

JOURNAL

Genesis 30:31–43

REFLECT AND WRITE.

- How did Laban respond to Jacob's request? How did Jacob use what he was given to his advantage?

- Do you think it was right that Jacob became extremely prosperous (see v. 43)? Why or why not? What personal application is there for you in this passage? How can you be assured that God is working behind the scenes in your life?

there. So the weaker animals ended up belonging to Laban and the stronger animals to Jacob. ⁴³ In this way Jacob became extremely prosperous. He owned large flocks, male and female servants, camels, and donkeys.

JACOB'S FLIGHT FROM LABAN

31 Jacob heard that Laban's sons were complaining, "Jacob has taken everything that belonged to our father! He has gotten rich at our father's expense!" ² When Jacob saw the look on Laban's face, he could tell his attitude toward him had changed.

³ The LORD said to Jacob, "Return to the land of your fathers and to your relatives. I will be with you." ⁴ So Jacob sent a message for Rachel and Leah to come to the field where his flocks were. ⁵ There he said to them, "I can tell that your father's attitude toward me has changed, but the God of my father has been with me. ⁶ You know that I've worked for your father as hard as I could, ⁷ but your father has humiliated me and changed my wages ten times. But God has not permitted him to do me any harm. ⁸ If he said, 'The speckled animals will be your wage,' then the entire flock gave birth to speckled offspring. But if he said, 'The streaked animals will be your wage,' then the entire flock gave birth to streaked offspring. ⁹ In this way God has snatched away your father's livestock and given them to me.

¹⁰ "Once during breeding season I saw in a dream that the male goats mating with the flock were streaked, speckled, and spotted. ¹¹ In the dream the angel of God said to me, 'Jacob!' 'Here I am!' I replied. ¹² Then he said, 'Observe that all the male goats mating with the flock are streaked, speckled, or spotted, for I have observed all that Laban has done to you. ¹³ I am the God of Bethel, where you anointed the sacred stone and made a vow to me. Now leave this land immediately and return to your native land.'"

¹⁴ Then Rachel and Leah replied to him, "Do we still have any portion or inheritance in our father's house? ¹⁵ Hasn't he treated us like foreigners? He not only sold us, but completely wasted the money paid for us! ¹⁶ Surely all the wealth that God snatched away from our father belongs to us and to our children. So now do everything God has told you."

PRAYING
SCRIPTURE

Genesis 31:1–13

This passage says Laban continued to deceive Jacob and oppose him. And yet God was caring for Jacob (v. 5). In what ways did God speak to Jacob, and how did He protect Jacob's interests? Pray that God would help you endure challenging situations by trusting God to provide for you. Recount the ways God has been with you in the past.

Also notice how Jacob responded to God (v. 11): he did not ignore God's instruction. The angel encouraged Jacob not to focus on his problems but to observe what God had done (v. 12) and recognize His presence. In prayer, lift up your eyes to God.

[17] So Jacob immediately put his children and his wives on the camels. [18] He took away all the livestock he had acquired in Paddan Aram and all his moveable property that he had accumulated. Then he set out toward the land of Canaan to return to his father Isaac.

[19] While Laban had gone to shear his sheep, Rachel stole the household idols that belonged to her father. [20] Jacob also deceived Laban the Aramean by not telling him that he was leaving. [21] He left with all he owned. He quickly crossed the Euphrates River and headed for the hill country of Gilead.

[22] Three days later Laban discovered Jacob had left. [23] So he took his relatives with him and pursued Jacob for seven days. He caught up with him in the hill country of Gilead. [24] But God came to Laban the Aramean in a dream at night and warned him, "Be careful that you neither bless nor curse Jacob."

[25] Laban overtook Jacob, and when Jacob pitched his tent in the hill country of Gilead, Laban and his relatives set up camp there too. [26] "What have you done?" Laban demanded of Jacob. "You've deceived me and carried away my daughters as if they were captives of war! [27] Why did you run away secretly and deceive me? Why didn't you tell me so I could send you off with a celebration complete with singing, tambourines, and harps? [28] You didn't even allow me to kiss my daughters and my grandchildren goodbye. You have acted foolishly! [29] I have the power to do you harm, but the God of your father told me last night, 'Be careful that you neither bless nor curse Jacob.' [30] Now I understand that you have gone away because you longed desperately for your father's house. Yet why did you steal my gods?"

[31] "I left secretly because I was afraid!" Jacob replied to Laban. "I thought you might take your daughters away from me by force. [32] Whoever has taken your gods will be put to death! In the presence of our relatives identify whatever is yours and take it." (Now Jacob did not know that Rachel had stolen them.)

[33] So Laban entered Jacob's tent, and Leah's tent, and the tent of the two female servants, but he did not find the idols. Then he left Leah's tent and entered Rachel's. [34] (Now Rachel had taken the idols and put them inside her camel's saddle

CONTEMPLATE

Genesis 31:22–42

READ. Read this passage. Search for a word, phrase, or verse to dwell on. Consider "Be careful that you neither bless nor curse Jacob" (v. 24) or "God saw how I was oppressed" (v. 42).

MEDITATE. How did God see Jacob through his years and years of toil? How will you use this account in the future to remind you that God sees you during difficult or lonely situations?

PRAY. The Hebrew name *El Roi* means "the God who sees me" (Gen 16:13). Thank God that His nature is unchanging. He saw Hagar by the spring, He saw Jacob during his faithful laboring, and He sees you too, wherever you are and whatever you are going through.

CONTEMPLATE. Spend a moment in quiet thanksgiving for His care for you.

and sat on them.) Laban searched the whole tent, but did not find them. 35 Rachel said to her father, "Don't be angry, my lord. I cannot stand up in your presence because I am having my period." So he searched thoroughly, but did not find the idols.

36 Jacob became angry and argued with Laban. "What did I do wrong?" he demanded of Laban. "What sin of mine prompted you to chase after me in hot pursuit? 37 When you searched through all my goods, did you find anything that belonged to you? Set it here before my relatives and yours, and let them settle the dispute between the two of us!

38 "I have been with you for the past twenty years. Your ewes and female goats have not miscarried, nor have I eaten rams from your flocks. 39 Animals torn by wild beasts I never brought to you; I always absorbed the loss myself. You always made me pay for every missing animal, whether it was taken by day or at night. 40 I was consumed by scorching heat during the day and by piercing cold at night, and I went without sleep. 41 This was my lot for twenty years in your house: I worked like a slave for you—fourteen years for your two daughters and six years for your flocks—but you changed my wages ten times! 42 If the God of my father—the God of Abraham, the one whom Isaac fears—had not been with me, you would certainly have sent me away empty-handed! But God saw how I was oppressed and how hard I worked, and he rebuked you last night."

43 Laban replied to Jacob, "These women are my daughters, these children are my grandchildren, and these flocks are my flocks. All that you see belongs to me. But how can I harm these daughters of mine today or the children to whom they have given birth? 44 So now, come, let's make a formal agreement, you and I, and it will be proof that we have made peace."

45 So Jacob took a stone and set it up as a memorial pillar. 46 Then he said to his relatives, "Gather stones." So they brought stones and put them in a pile. They ate there by the pile of stones. 47 Laban called it Jegar Sahadutha, but Jacob called it Galeed.

JOURNAL

Genesis 31:45–55

REFLECT AND WRITE.

- What was the purpose of setting up a stone pillar? How did it serve as a reminder of the covenant between Laban and Jacob?

- What might God want to say to you today? How do you need to symbolize something in your life to remember it and keep any promises you've made?

⁴⁸ Laban said, "This pile of stones is a witness of our agreement today." That is why it was called Galeed. ⁴⁹ It was also called Mizpah because he said, "May the LORD watch between us when we are out of sight of one another. ⁵⁰ If you mistreat my daughters or if you take wives besides my daughters, although no one else is with us, realize that God is witness to your actions."

⁵¹ "Here is this pile of stones and this pillar I have set up between me and you," Laban said to Jacob. ⁵² "This pile of stones and the pillar are reminders that I will not pass beyond this pile to come to harm you and that you will not pass beyond this pile and this pillar to come to harm me. ⁵³ May the God of Abraham and the god of Nahor, the gods of their father, judge between us." Jacob took an oath by the God whom his father Isaac feared. ⁵⁴ Then Jacob offered a sacrifice on the mountain and invited his relatives to eat the meal. They ate the meal and spent the night on the mountain.

⁵⁵ Early in the morning Laban kissed his grandchildren and his daughters goodbye and blessed them. Then Laban left and returned home.

JACOB WRESTLES AT PENIEL

32 So Jacob went on his way and the angels of God met him. ² When Jacob saw them, he exclaimed, "This is the camp of God!" So he named that place Mahanaim.

³ Jacob sent messengers on ahead to his brother Esau in the land of Seir, the region of Edom. ⁴ He commanded them, "This is what you must say to my lord Esau: 'This is what your servant Jacob says: I have been staying with Laban until now. ⁵ I have oxen, donkeys, sheep, and male and female servants. I have sent this message to inform my lord, so that I may find favor in your sight.'"

⁶ The messengers returned to Jacob and said, "We went to your brother Esau. He is coming to meet you and has 400 men with him." ⁷ Jacob was very afraid and upset. So he divided the people who were with him into two camps, as well as the flocks, herds, and camels. ⁸ "If Esau attacks one camp," he thought, "then the other camp will be able to escape."

Genesis 32:6–12

Jacob was afraid that Esau would attack his family, so he prayed for God's protection. He recognized he did not deserve God's favor (v. 10). After all, Jacob had deceived his father in order to claim Esau's birthright. Due to his sin, he might have wondered if God would listen to his prayer. Nevertheless, he remembered God's promises to him. Those promises gave him confidence to ask God to protect him from Esau.

Pray the words in Genesis 32:9–12. How has God shown you mercy? Remember that God's grace through Jesus gives you the opportunity to pray (Rom 5:1–2). Boldly ask for God's continued deliverance from your enemies.

⁹Then Jacob prayed, "O God of my father Abraham, God of my father Isaac, O LORD, you said to me, 'Return to your land and to your relatives and I will make you prosper.' ¹⁰I am not worthy of all the faithful love you have shown your servant. With only my walking stick I crossed the Jordan, but now I have become two camps. ¹¹Rescue me, I pray, from the hand of my brother Esau, for I am afraid he will come and attack me, as well as the mothers with their children. ¹²But you said, 'I will certainly make you prosper and will make your descendants like the sand on the seashore, too numerous to count.'"

¹³Jacob stayed there that night. Then he sent as a gift to his brother Esau ¹⁴200 female goats and 20 male goats, 200 ewes and 20 rams, ¹⁵30 female camels with their young, 40 cows and 10 bulls, and 20 female donkeys and 10 male donkeys. ¹⁶He entrusted them to his servants, who divided them into herds. He told his servants, "Pass over before me, and keep some distance between one herd and the next." ¹⁷He instructed the servant leading the first herd, "When my brother Esau meets you and asks, 'To whom do you belong? Where are you going? Whose herds are you driving?' ¹⁸then you must say, 'They belong to your servant Jacob. They have been sent as a gift to my lord Esau. In fact Jacob himself is behind us.'"

¹⁹He also gave these instructions to the second and third servants, as well as all those who were following the herds, saying, "You must say the same thing to Esau when you meet him. ²⁰You must also say, 'In fact your servant Jacob is behind us.'" Jacob thought, "I will first appease him by sending a gift ahead of me. After that I will meet him. Perhaps he will accept me." ²¹So the gifts were sent on ahead of him while he spent that night in the camp.

²²During the night Jacob quickly took his two wives, his two female servants, and his eleven sons and crossed the ford of the Jabbok. ²³He took them and sent them across the stream along with all his possessions. ²⁴So Jacob was left alone. Then a man wrestled with him until daybreak. ²⁵When the man saw that he could not defeat Jacob, he struck the socket of his hip so the socket of Jacob's hip was dislocated while he wrestled with him.

PICTURE IT

Genesis 32:24–32

PICTURE. As you read the verses, what comes to mind? Imagine you're alone after having been surrounded by people for weeks. How does this feel? What do you picture the man to look like? Draw a brief sketch if you can. Now picture the wrestling match—the sounds, smells, and struggle. Why doesn't the man just destroy Jacob? How does Jacob look, feel, even smell after wrestling all night? If you were Jacob, would you feel victorious, as your new name, Israel, suggests? Imagine Jacob's walking with a limp. How does this affect his journey?

PRAY. Pray about your own "wrestling matches" with God. Ask God to reveal to you a deeper understanding of His heart, character, and love.

²⁶Then the man said, "Let me go, for the dawn is breaking." "I will not let you go," Jacob replied, "unless you bless me." ²⁷The man asked him, "What is your name?" He answered, "Jacob." ²⁸"No longer will your name be Jacob," the man told him, "but Israel, because you have fought with God and with men and have prevailed."

²⁹Then Jacob asked, "Please tell me your name." "Why do you ask my name?" the man replied. Then he blessed Jacob there. ³⁰So Jacob named the place Peniel, explaining, "Certainly I have seen God face to face and have survived."

³¹The sun rose over him as he crossed over Penuel, but he was limping because of his hip. ³²That is why to this day the Israelites do not eat the sinew which is attached to the socket of the hip, because he struck the socket of Jacob's hip near the attached sinew.

JACOB MEETS ESAU

33 Jacob looked up and saw that Esau was coming along with 400 men. So he divided the children among Leah, Rachel, and the two female servants. ²He put the servants and their children in front, with Leah and her children behind them, and Rachel and Joseph behind them. ³But Jacob himself went on ahead of them, and he bowed toward the ground seven times as he approached his brother. ⁴But Esau ran to meet him, embraced him, hugged his neck, and kissed him. Then they both wept. ⁵When Esau looked up and saw the women and the children, he asked, "Who are these people with you?" Jacob replied, "The children whom God has graciously given your servant." ⁶The female servants came forward with their children and bowed down. ⁷Then Leah came forward with her children and they bowed down. Finally Joseph and Rachel came forward and bowed down.

⁸Esau then asked, "What did you intend by sending all these herds to meet me?" Jacob replied, "To find favor in your sight, my lord." ⁹But Esau said, "I have plenty, my brother. Keep what belongs to you." ¹⁰"No, please take them," Jacob said. "If I have found favor in your sight, accept my gift from my hand. Now that I have seen your face and you have accepted me, it is as

CONTEMPLATE

Genesis 33:1–11

READ. Keep Jacob and Esau's last encounter in mind (Gen 27:41–45) as you read these verses. Choose a verse to meditate on, perhaps verse 4 or 11. Linger with the verse a few times to absorb its meaning and context.

MEDITATE. Have you ever expected the worst but were pleasantly surprised by the outcome? Has God dealt graciously with you (v. 11)? What does the Spirit say to you through this passage? Ask Him to bring things to mind, and then allow Him a moment to do so.

PRAY. Pray that God will open your eyes to His works of grace in your life. Pray that you will show others the same grace and forgiveness God has shown you (Eph 4:32).

CONTEMPLATE. Determine how to live out Colossians 4:6: "Let your speech always be gracious."

if I have seen the face of God. ¹¹ Please take my present that was brought to you, for God has been generous to me and I have all I need." When Jacob urged him, he took it.

¹² Then Esau said, "Let's be on our way! I will go in front of you." ¹³ But Jacob said to him, "My lord knows that the children are young, and that I have to look after the sheep and cattle that are nursing their young. If they are driven too hard for even a single day, all the animals will die. ¹⁴ Let my lord go on ahead of his servant. I will travel more slowly, at the pace of the herds and the children, until I come to my lord at Seir."

¹⁵ So Esau said, "Let me leave some of my men with you." "Why do that?" Jacob replied. "My lord has already been kind enough to me."

¹⁶ So that same day Esau made his way back to Seir. ¹⁷ But Jacob traveled to Sukkoth where he built himself a house and made shelters for his livestock. That is why the place was called Sukkoth.

¹⁸ After he left Paddan Aram, Jacob came safely to the city of Shechem in the land of Canaan, and he camped near the city. ¹⁹ Then he purchased the portion of the field where he had pitched his tent; he bought it from the sons of Hamor, Shechem's father, for 100 pieces of money. ²⁰ There he set up an altar and called it "The God of Israel is God."

DINAH AND THE SHECHEMITES

34 Now Dinah, Leah's daughter whom she bore to Jacob, went to meet the young women of the land. ² When Shechem son of Hamor the Hivite, who ruled that area, saw her, he grabbed her, forced himself on her, and sexually assaulted her. ³ Then he became very attached to Dinah, Jacob's daughter. He fell in love with the young woman and spoke romantically to her. ⁴ Shechem said to his father Hamor, "Acquire this young girl as my wife." ⁵ When Jacob heard that Shechem had violated his daughter Dinah, his sons were with the livestock in the field. So Jacob remained silent until they came in.

⁶ Then Shechem's father Hamor went to speak with Jacob about Dinah. ⁷ Now Jacob's sons had come in from the field when they heard the news. They were offended and very angry

JOURNAL

Genesis 34:1–17

REFLECT AND WRITE.

- How would you summarize this passage to help clarify the details?

- How were Jacob's sons deceitful toward Shechem and Hamor (see v. 13)? Why was it wrong for Dinah to marry an uncircumcised man?

- When have you seen situations like this (sexual abuse, harassment, deceit, bait-and-switch tactics)? How can you avoid being jaded by what you see? How can you avoid being "conformed to this present world" (Rom 12:2) related to those matters?

because Shechem had disgraced Israel by sexually assaulting Jacob's daughter, a crime that should not be committed.

⁸But Hamor made this appeal to them: "My son Shechem is in love with your daughter. Please give her to him as his wife. ⁹Intermarry with us. Let us marry your daughters, and take our daughters as wives for yourselves. ¹⁰You may live among us, and the land will be open to you. Live in it, travel freely in it, and acquire property in it."

¹¹Then Shechem said to Dinah's father and brothers, "Let me find favor in your sight, and whatever you require of me I'll give. ¹²You can make the bride price and the gift I must bring very expensive, and I'll give whatever you ask of me. Just give me the young woman as my wife!"

¹³Jacob's sons answered Shechem and his father Hamor deceitfully when they spoke because Shechem had violated their sister Dinah. ¹⁴They said to them, "We cannot give our sister to a man who is not circumcised, for it would be a disgrace to us. ¹⁵We will give you our consent on this one condition: You must become like us by circumcising all your males. ¹⁶Then we will give you our daughters to marry, and we will take your daughters as wives for ourselves, and we will live among you and become one people. ¹⁷But if you do not agree to our terms by being circumcised, then we will take our sister and depart."

¹⁸Their offer pleased Hamor and his son Shechem. ¹⁹The young man did not delay in doing what they asked because he wanted Jacob's daughter Dinah badly. (Now he was more important than anyone in his father's household.) ²⁰So Hamor and his son Shechem went to the gate of their city and spoke to the men of their city, ²¹"These men are at peace with us. So let them live in the land and travel freely in it, for the land is wide enough for them. We will take their daughters for wives, and we will give them our daughters to marry. ²²Only on this one condition will these men consent to live with us and become one people: They demand that every male among us be circumcised just as they are circumcised. ²³If we do so, won't their livestock, their property, and all their animals become ours? So let's consent to their demand, so they will live among us."

²⁴ All the men who assembled at the city gate agreed with Hamor and his son Shechem. Every male who assembled at the city gate was circumcised. ²⁵ In three days, when they were still in pain, two of Jacob's sons, Simeon and Levi, Dinah's brothers, each took his sword and went to the unsuspecting city and slaughtered every male. ²⁶ They killed Hamor and his son Shechem with the sword, took Dinah from Shechem's house, and left. ²⁷ Jacob's sons killed them and looted the city because their sister had been violated. ²⁸ They took their flocks, herds, and donkeys, as well as everything in the city and in the surrounding fields. ²⁹ They captured as plunder all their wealth, all their little ones, and their wives, including everything in the houses.

³⁰ Then Jacob said to Simeon and Levi, "You have brought ruin on me by making me a foul odor among the inhabitants of the land—among the Canaanites and the Perizzites. I am few in number; they will join forces against me and attack me, and both I and my family will be destroyed!" ³¹ But Simeon and Levi replied, "Should he treat our sister like a common prostitute?"

THE RETURN TO BETHEL

35 Then God said to Jacob, "Go up at once to Bethel and live there. Make an altar there to God, who appeared to you when you fled from your brother Esau." ² So Jacob told his household and all who were with him, "Get rid of the foreign gods you have among you. Purify yourselves and change your clothes. ³ Let us go up at once to Bethel. Then I will make an altar there to God, who responded to me in my time of distress and has been with me wherever I went."

⁴ So they gave Jacob all the foreign gods that were in their possession and the rings that were in their ears. Jacob buried them under the oak near Shechem ⁵ and they started on their journey. The surrounding cities were afraid of God, and they did not pursue the sons of Jacob.

⁶ Jacob and all those who were with him arrived at Luz (that is, Bethel) in the land of Canaan. ⁷ He built an altar there and named the place El Bethel because there God had revealed

CONTEMPLATE

Genesis 34:25–31

READ. Read the passage twice. Take some time to meditate on verse 30 in particular. Repeat it as you seek to understand its meaning and importance in context.

MEDITATE. Can you relate to or empathize with Jacob's predicament? Have you ever felt as if everyone was against you? If so, how did you handle it at the time? How has this kind of experience influenced your spiritual journey?

PRAY. Ask God to help you face situations like Jacob's in which any hope of peace disappears. How can you allow God to fight your battles for you today? Ask Him to be your strength and shield no matter what you face (Ps 28:7).

CONTEMPLATE. Let your heart greatly rejoice in the Lord who helps you. Then praise Him with song.

 PRAYING
SCRIPTURE

Genesis 35:1–7

Jacob and his family had been living among people who worshiped false gods, and idols had infiltrated his family. After God appeared and spoke to him, Jacob called on his family members to expel all the idols, which they did. Ask God to speak to you through His Word about possible idolatry in your life or family. Are there idols to expel from your life—relationships, activities, or possessions that claim your devotion and take priority over God? Ask God to help you devote your life completely to Him.

himself to him when he was fleeing from his brother. 8 (Deborah, Rebekah's nurse, died and was buried under the oak below Bethel; thus it was named Oak of Weeping.)

9 God appeared to Jacob again after he returned from Paddan Aram and blessed him. 10 God said to him, "Your name is Jacob, but your name will no longer be called Jacob; Israel will be your name." So God named him Israel. 11 Then God said to him, "I am the Sovereign God. Be fruitful and multiply! A nation—even a company of nations—will descend from you; kings will be among your descendants! 12 The land I gave to Abraham and Isaac I will give to you. To your descendants I will also give this land." 13 Then God went up from the place where he spoke with him. 14 So Jacob set up a sacred stone pillar in the place where God spoke with him. He poured out a drink offering on it, and then he poured oil on it. 15 Jacob named the place where God spoke with him Bethel.

16 They traveled on from Bethel, and when Ephrath was still some distance away, Rachel went into labor—and her labor was hard. 17 When her labor was at its hardest, the midwife said to her, "Don't be afraid, for you are having another son." 18 With her dying breath, she named him Ben Oni. But his father called him Benjamin instead. 19 So Rachel died and was buried on the way to Ephrath (that is, Bethlehem). 20 Jacob set up a marker over her grave; it is the Marker of Rachel's Grave to this day.

21 Then Israel traveled on and pitched his tent beyond Migdal Eder. 22 While Israel was living in that land, Reuben went to bed with Bilhah, his father's concubine, and Israel heard about it.

Jacob had twelve sons:

23   The sons of Leah were Reuben, Jacob's firstborn, as
         well as Simeon, Levi, Judah, Issachar, and Zebulun.
24   The sons of Rachel were Joseph and Benjamin.
25   The sons of Bilhah, Rachel's servant,
         were Dan and Naphtali.
26   The sons of Zilpah, Leah's servant, were Gad and Asher.

These were the sons of Jacob who were born to him in Paddan Aram.

Genesis 35:10–15

READ. Read the passage and consider the phrase "I am the Sovereign God" (v. 11). Meditate on these words for a moment.

MEDITATE. Notice that God gave Jacob a new command along with his new name (vv. 10–11). Consider again the phrase "I am the Sovereign God." In light of verses 10–11, how does this phrase encourage or convict you?

PRAY. Bring your convictions and responses to God in prayer. Praise God that He alone is sovereign. Pray that this truth strengthens your resolve to keep faith in Him.

CONTEMPLATE. Proverbs 18:10 says, "The name of the LORD is like a strong tower; the righteous person runs to it and is set safely on high." Clear your mind of worries and distractions, and be still in God's holy and loving presence.

²⁷ So Jacob came back to his father Isaac in Mamre, to Kiriath Arba (that is, Hebron), where Abraham and Isaac had stayed. ²⁸ Isaac lived to be 180 years old. ²⁹ Then Isaac breathed his last and joined his ancestors. He died an old man who had lived a full life. His sons Esau and Jacob buried him.

THE DESCENDANTS OF ESAU

36 What follows is the account of Esau (also known as Edom).

² Esau took his wives from the Canaanites: Adah the daughter of Elon the Hittite, and Oholibamah the daughter of Anah and granddaughter of Zibeon the Hivite, ³ in addition to Basemath the daughter of Ishmael and sister of Nebaioth.

⁴ Adah bore Eliphaz to Esau, Basemath bore Reuel, ⁵ and Oholibamah bore Jeush, Jalam, and Korah. These were the sons of Esau who were born to him in the land of Canaan.

⁶ Esau took his wives, his sons, his daughters, all the people in his household, his livestock, his animals, and all his possessions that he had acquired in the land of Canaan, and he went to a land some distance away from Jacob his brother ⁷ because they had too many possessions to be able to stay together, and the land where they had settled was not able to support them because of their livestock. ⁸ So Esau (also known as Edom) lived in the hill country of Seir.

⁹ This is the account of Esau, the father of the Edomites, in the hill country of Seir.

¹⁰ These were the names of Esau's sons: Eliphaz, the son of Esau's wife Adah, and Reuel, the son of Esau's wife Basemath.

¹¹ These were the sons of Eliphaz: Teman, Omar, Zepho, Gatam, and Kenaz.

¹² Timna, a concubine of Esau's son Eliphaz, bore Amalek to Eliphaz. These were the sons of Esau's wife Adah.

¹³ These were the sons of Reuel: Nahath, Zerah, Shammah, and Mizzah. These were the sons of Esau's wife Basemath.

¹⁴ These were the sons of Esau's wife Oholibamah the daughter of Anah and granddaughter of Zibeon: She bore Jeush, Jalam, and Korah to Esau.

¹⁵ These were the chiefs among the descendants of Esau, the sons of Eliphaz, Esau's firstborn: chief Teman, chief Omar, chief Zepho, chief Kenaz, ¹⁶ chief Korah, chief Gatam, chief Amalek. These were the chiefs descended from Eliphaz in the land of Edom; these were the sons of Adah.

¹⁷ These were the sons of Esau's son Reuel: chief Nahath, chief Zerah, chief Shammah, chief Mizzah. These were the chiefs descended from Reuel in the land of Edom; these were the sons of Esau's wife Basemath.

¹⁸ These were the sons of Esau's wife Oholibamah: chief Jeush, chief Jalam, chief Korah. These were the chiefs descended from Esau's wife Oholibamah, the daughter of Anah.

¹⁹ These were the sons of Esau (also known as Edom), and these were their chiefs.

²⁰ These were the sons of Seir the Horite, who were living in the land: Lotan, Shobal, Zibeon, Anah, ²¹ Dishon, Ezer, and Dishan. These were the chiefs of the Horites, the descendants of Seir in the land of Edom.

²² The sons of Lotan were Hori and Homam; Lotan's sister was Timna.

²³ These were the sons of Shobal: Alvan, Manahath, Ebal, Shepho, and Onam.

²⁴ These were the sons of Zibeon: Aiah and Anah (who discovered the hot springs in the wilderness as he pastured the donkeys of his father Zibeon).

²⁵ These were the children of Anah: Dishon and Oholibamah, the daughter of Anah.

²⁶ These were the sons of Dishon: Hemdan, Eshban, Ithran, and Keran.

²⁷ These were the sons of Ezer: Bilhan, Zaavan, and Akan.

²⁸ These were the sons of Dishan: Uz and Aran.

²⁹ These were the chiefs of the Horites: chief Lotan, chief Shobal, chief Zibeon, chief Anah, ³⁰ chief Dishon, chief Ezer, chief Dishan. These were the chiefs of the Horites, according to their chief lists in the land of Seir.

[31]These were the kings who reigned in the land of Edom before any king ruled over the Israelites:

[32]Bela the son of Beor reigned in Edom; the name of his city was Dinhabah.

[33]When Bela died, Jobab the son of Zerah from Bozrah reigned in his place.

[34]When Jobab died, Husham from the land of the Temanites reigned in his place.

[35]When Husham died, Hadad the son of Bedad, who defeated the Midianites in the land of Moab, reigned in his place; the name of his city was Avith.

[36]When Hadad died, Samlah from Masrekah reigned in his place.

[37]When Samlah died, Shaul from Rehoboth on the River reigned in his place.

[38]When Shaul died, Baal Hanan the son of Achbor reigned in his place.

[39]When Baal Hanan the son of Achbor died, Hadad reigned in his place; the name of his city was Pau. His wife's name was Mehetabel, the daughter of Matred, the daughter of Me-Zahab.

[40]These were the names of the chiefs of Esau, according to their families, according to their places, by their names: chief Timna, chief Alvah, chief Jetheth, [41]chief Oholibamah, chief Elah, chief Pinon, [42]chief Kenaz, chief Teman, chief Mibzar, [43]chief Magdiel, chief Iram. These were the chiefs of Edom, according to their settlements in the land they possessed. This was Esau, the father of the Edomites.

JOSEPH'S DREAMS

37 But Jacob lived in the land where his father had stayed, in the land of Canaan.

[2]This is the account of Jacob.

Joseph, his seventeen-year-old son, was taking care of the flocks with his brothers. Now he was a youngster working with the sons of Bilhah and Zilpah, his father's wives. Joseph brought back a bad report about them to their father.

JOURNAL

Genesis 37:2–11

REFLECT AND WRITE.

- If you had been a son of Jacob (Israel), would you have wanted to be Joseph? Why or why not?

- Summarize Joseph's dreams. How did his father and brothers respond when Joseph told them about his dreams? How did their responses differ?

- Based on what you know of his story, was Joseph wrong to share his dream with his family (see Gen 42:6)? Why is Joseph's story important in the overall biblical narrative?

³ Now Israel loved Joseph more than all his sons because he was a son born to him late in life, and he made a special tunic for him. ⁴ When Joseph's brothers saw that their father loved him more than any of them, they hated Joseph and were not able to speak to him kindly.

⁵ Joseph had a dream, and when he told his brothers about it they hated him even more. ⁶ He said to them, "Listen to this dream I had: ⁷ There we were, binding sheaves of grain in the middle of the field. Suddenly my sheaf rose up and stood upright and your sheaves surrounded my sheaf and bowed down to it!" ⁸ Then his brothers asked him, "Do you really think you will rule over us or have dominion over us?" They hated him even more because of his dream and because of what he said.

⁹ Then he had another dream, and told it to his brothers. "Look," he said. "I had another dream. The sun, the moon, and eleven stars were bowing down to me." ¹⁰ When he told his father and his brothers, his father rebuked him, saying, "What is this dream that you had? Will I, your mother, and your brothers really come and bow down to you?" ¹¹ His brothers were jealous of him, but his father kept in mind what Joseph said.

¹² When his brothers had gone to graze their father's flocks near Shechem, ¹³ Israel said to Joseph, "Your brothers are grazing the flocks near Shechem. Come, I will send you to them." "I'm ready," Joseph replied. ¹⁴ So Jacob said to him, "Go now and check on the welfare of your brothers and of the flocks, and bring me word." So Jacob sent him from the valley of Hebron.

¹⁵ When Joseph reached Shechem, a man found him wandering in the field, so the man asked him, "What are you looking for?" ¹⁶ He replied, "I'm looking for my brothers. Please tell me where they are grazing their flocks." ¹⁷ The man said, "They left this area, for I heard them say, 'Let's go to Dothan.'" So Joseph went after his brothers and found them at Dothan.

¹⁸ Now Joseph's brothers saw him from a distance, and before he reached them, they plotted to kill him. ¹⁹ They said to one another, "Here comes this master of dreams! ²⁰ Come now, let's kill him, throw him into one of the cisterns, and then say that a wild animal ate him. Then we'll see how his dreams turn out!"

 CONTEMPLATE

Genesis 37:12–28

READ. Read these verses twice. Choose one verse to meditate on, such as verse 13 or 28. Repeat this verse and seek to understand its importance in Joseph's story.

MEDITATE. How did God position Joseph as a part of His greater plan? How does this part of Joseph's life reflect what we read in Romans 8:28? Does this give you hope in God's plan for your life? Take heart and remember that the light of Christ shines bright in the darkest situations.

PRAY. Turn your thoughts to prayer. Praise God that His plans are good. Ask Him to reveal where He is at work in a place you may not yet perceive Him to be.

CONTEMPLATE. Allow the Spirit to guide you as you quietly reflect on God's providence.

²¹When Reuben heard this, he rescued Joseph from their hands, saying, "Let's not take his life!" ²²Reuben continued, "Don't shed blood! Throw him into this cistern that is here in the wilderness, but don't lay a hand on him." (Reuben said this so he could rescue Joseph from them and take him back to his father.)

²³When Joseph reached his brothers, they stripped him of his tunic, the special tunic that he wore. ²⁴Then they took him and threw him into the cistern. (Now the cistern was empty; there was no water in it.)

²⁵When they sat down to eat their food, they looked up and saw a caravan of Ishmaelites coming from Gilead. Their camels were carrying spices, balm, and myrrh down to Egypt. ²⁶Then Judah said to his brothers, "What profit is there if we kill our brother and cover up his blood? ²⁷Come, let's sell him to the Ishmaelites, but let's not lay a hand on him, for after all, he is our brother, our own flesh." His brothers agreed. ²⁸So when the Midianite merchants passed by, Joseph's brothers pulled him out of the cistern and sold him to the Ishmaelites for twenty pieces of silver. The Ishmaelites then took Joseph to Egypt.

²⁹Later Reuben returned to the cistern to find that Joseph was not in it! He tore his clothes, ³⁰returned to his brothers, and said, "The boy isn't there! And I, where can I go?" ³¹So they took Joseph's tunic, killed a young goat, and dipped the tunic in the blood. ³²Then they brought the special tunic to their father and said, "We found this. Determine now whether it is your son's tunic or not."

³³He recognized it and exclaimed, "It is my son's tunic! A wild animal has eaten him! Joseph has surely been torn to pieces!" ³⁴Then Jacob tore his clothes, put on sackcloth, and mourned for his son many days. ³⁵All his sons and daughters stood by him to console him, but he refused to be consoled. "No," he said, "I will go to the grave mourning my son." So Joseph's father wept for him.

³⁶Now in Egypt the Midianites sold Joseph to Potiphar, one of Pharaoh's officials, the captain of the guard.

PRAYING SCRIPTURE

Genesis 37:31–35

For a parent, it is hard to imagine anything harder in life than the death of a son or daughter. This passage portrays a suffering father who *thought* his son was dead. Jacob mourned many days and could not be comforted by the people in his life (vv. 34–35). His son Joseph, however, was alive. At the time, Jacob did not know God's larger plan.

Do you believe God is working through pain and suffering? When you experience loss, pray for peace, comfort, and hope. And pray that God would help you bring comfort to those who are dealing with sorrow.

JUDAH AND TAMAR

38 At that time Judah left his brothers and stayed with an Adullamite man named Hirah. ² There Judah saw the daughter of a Canaanite man named Shua. Judah acquired her as a wife and slept with her. ³ She became pregnant and had a son. Judah named him Er. ⁴ She became pregnant again and had another son, whom she named Onan. ⁵ Then she had yet another son, whom she named Shelah. She gave birth to him in Kezib.

⁶ Judah acquired a wife for Er his firstborn; her name was Tamar. ⁷ But Er, Judah's firstborn, was evil in the LORD's sight, so the LORD killed him.

⁸ Then Judah said to Onan, "Sleep with your brother's wife and fulfill the duty of a brother-in-law to her so that you may raise up a descendant for your brother." ⁹ But Onan knew that the child would not be considered his. So whenever he slept with his brother's wife, he wasted his emission on the ground so as not to give his brother a descendant. ¹⁰ What he did was evil in the LORD's sight, so the LORD killed him too.

¹¹ Then Judah said to his daughter-in-law Tamar, "Live as a widow in your father's house until Shelah my son grows up." For he thought, "I don't want him to die like his brothers." So Tamar went and lived in her father's house.

¹² After some time Judah's wife, the daughter of Shua, died. After Judah was consoled, he left for Timnah to visit his sheep-shearers, along with his friend Hirah the Adullamite. ¹³ Tamar was told, "Look, your father-in-law is going up to Timnah to shear his sheep." ¹⁴ So she removed her widow's clothes and covered herself with a veil. She wrapped herself and sat at the entrance to Enaim which is on the way to Timnah. (She did this because she saw that she had not been given to Shelah as a wife, even though he had now grown up.)

¹⁵ When Judah saw her, he thought she was a prostitute because she had covered her face. ¹⁶ He turned aside to her along the road and said, "Come, please, I want to sleep with you." (He did not realize it was his daughter-in-law.) She asked, "What will you give me so that you may sleep with me?" ¹⁷ He replied, "I'll send you a young goat from the flock." She asked, "Will you

give me a pledge until you send it?" 18 He said, "What pledge should I give you?" She replied, "Your seal, your cord, and the staff that's in your hand." So he gave them to her, then slept with her, and she became pregnant by him. 19 She left immediately, removed her veil, and put on her widow's clothes.

20 Then Judah had his friend Hirah the Adullamite take a young goat to get back from the woman the items he had given in pledge, but Hirah could not find her. 21 He asked the men who were there, "Where is the cult prostitute who was at Enaim by the road?" But they replied, "There has been no cult prostitute here." 22 So he returned to Judah and said, "I couldn't find her. Moreover, the men of the place said, 'There has been no cult prostitute here.'" 23 Judah said, "Let her keep the things for herself. Otherwise we will appear to be dishonest. I did indeed send this young goat, but you couldn't find her."

24 After three months Judah was told, "Your daughter-in-law Tamar has turned to prostitution, and as a result she has become pregnant." Judah said, "Bring her out and let her be burned!" 25 While they were bringing her out, she sent word to her father-in-law: "I am pregnant by the man to whom these belong." Then she said, "Identify the one to whom the seal, cord, and staff belong." 26 Judah recognized them and said, "She is more upright than I am, because I wouldn't give her to Shelah my son." He was not physically intimate with her again.

27 When it was time for her to give birth, there were twins in her womb. 28 While she was giving birth, one child put out his hand, and the midwife took a scarlet thread and tied it on his hand, saying, "This one came out first." 29 But then he drew back his hand, and his brother came out before him. She said, "How you have broken out of the womb!" So he was named Perez. 30 Afterward his brother came out—the one who had the scarlet thread on his hand—and he was named Zerah.

JOSEPH AND POTIPHAR'S WIFE

39 Now Joseph had been brought down to Egypt. An Egyptian named Potiphar, an official of Pharaoh and the captain of the guard, purchased him from the Ishmaelites who had brought him there. 2 The LORD was with Joseph.

JOURNAL

Genesis 38:24–30

REFLECT AND WRITE.

- Compare Judah's characteristics and actions (see Gen 38) with Joseph's characteristics and actions (see Gen 39). Who do you want to be more like?

- Tamar gave birth to twin boys, Perez and Zerah (see vv. 29–30). How did God use the Judah and Tamar scandal to bring about redemption for humanity through Christ (see Matt 1:3)? What does this demonstrate about God and His redemptive work?

PRAYING SCRIPTURE

Genesis 39:1–6

Meditate on what it must have been like for Joseph in Egypt. His brothers had sold him into slavery. He was far from home in a foreign land, and he'd changed from favored son to lowly servant. Yet God was with Joseph and blessed him with favor in Potiphar's house (vv. 2, 4). God did not remove Joseph from his difficulties but helped Joseph *through* them.

How has the Lord been with you in situations that seemed hopeless? How does Joseph's story give you hope and courage? Ask God for help and wisdom to aid people who are suffering.

He was successful and lived in the household of his Egyptian master. ³ His master observed that the LORD was with him and that the LORD made everything he was doing successful. ⁴ So Joseph found favor in his sight and became his personal attendant. Potiphar appointed Joseph overseer of his household and put him in charge of everything he owned. ⁵ From the time Potiphar appointed him over his household and over all that he owned, the LORD blessed the Egyptian's household for Joseph's sake. The blessing of the LORD was on everything that he had, both in his house and in his fields. ⁶ So Potiphar left everything he had in Joseph's care; he gave no thought to anything except the food he ate.

Now Joseph was well built and good-looking. ⁷ Soon after these things, his master's wife took notice of Joseph and said, "Come to bed with me." ⁸ But he refused, saying to his master's wife, "Look, my master does not give any thought to his household with me here, and everything that he owns he has put into my care. ⁹ There is no one greater in this household than I am. He has withheld nothing from me except you because you are his wife. So how could I do such a great evil and sin against God?" ¹⁰ Even though she continued to speak to Joseph day after day, he did not respond to her invitation to go to bed with her.

¹¹ One day he went into the house to do his work when none of the household servants were there in the house. ¹² She grabbed him by his outer garment, saying, "Come to bed with me!" But he left his outer garment in her hand and ran outside. ¹³ When she saw that he had left his outer garment in her hand and had run outside, ¹⁴ she called for her household servants and said to them, "See, my husband brought in a Hebrew man to us to humiliate us. He tried to go to bed with me, but I screamed loudly. ¹⁵ When he heard me raise my voice and scream, he left his outer garment beside me and ran outside."

¹⁶ So she laid his outer garment beside her until his master came home. ¹⁷ This is what she said to him: "That Hebrew slave you brought to us tried to humiliate me, ¹⁸ but when I raised my voice and screamed, he left his outer garment and ran outside."

JOURNAL

Genesis 39:7–23

REFLECT AND WRITE.

- What characteristics does Joseph display in this passage? How can the Holy Spirit help you live out these character traits?

- How would you have felt if you had been thrown into prison like Joseph? What can you learn from Joseph's story (see vv. 20–23)?

¹⁹ When his master heard his wife say, "This is the way your slave treated me," he became furious. ²⁰ Joseph's master took him and threw him into the prison, the place where the king's prisoners were confined. So he was there in the prison.

²¹ But the LORD was with Joseph and showed him kindness. He granted him favor in the sight of the prison warden. ²² The warden put all the prisoners under Joseph's care. He was in charge of whatever they were doing. ²³ The warden did not concern himself with anything that was in Joseph's care because the LORD was with him and whatever he was doing the LORD was making successful.

THE CUPBEARER AND THE BAKER

40 After these things happened, the cupbearer to the king of Egypt and the royal baker offended their master, the king of Egypt. ² Pharaoh was enraged with his two officials, the cupbearer and the baker, ³ so he imprisoned them in the house of the captain of the guard in the same facility where Joseph was confined. ⁴ The captain of the guard appointed Joseph to be their attendant, and he served them.

They spent some time in custody. ⁵ Both of them, the cupbearer and the baker of the king of Egypt, who were confined in the prison, had a dream the same night. Each man's dream had its own meaning. ⁶ When Joseph came to them in the morning, he saw that they were looking depressed. ⁷ So he asked Pharaoh's officials, who were with him in custody in his master's house, "Why do you look so sad today?" ⁸ They told him, "We both had dreams, but there is no one to interpret them." Joseph responded, "Don't interpretations belong to God? Tell them to me."

⁹ So the chief cupbearer told his dream to Joseph: "In my dream, there was a vine in front of me. ¹⁰ On the vine there were three branches. As it budded, its blossoms opened and its clusters ripened into grapes. ¹¹ Now Pharaoh's cup was in my hand, so I took the grapes, squeezed them into his cup, and put the cup in Pharaoh's hand."

¹² "This is its meaning," Joseph said to him. "The three branches represent three days. ¹³ In three more days Pharaoh will reinstate you and restore you to your office. You will put Pharaoh's cup in his hand, just as you did before when you were cupbearer. ¹⁴ But remember me when it goes well for you, and show me kindness. Make mention of me to Pharaoh and bring me out of this prison, ¹⁵ for I really was kidnapped from the land of the Hebrews and I have done nothing wrong here for which they should put me in a dungeon."

¹⁶ When the chief baker saw that the interpretation of the first dream was favorable, he said to Joseph, "I also appeared in my dream and there were three baskets of white bread on my head. ¹⁷ In the top basket there were baked goods of every kind for Pharaoh, but the birds were eating them from the basket that was on my head."

¹⁸ Joseph replied, "This is its meaning: The three baskets represent three days. ¹⁹ In three more days Pharaoh will decapitate you and impale you on a pole. Then the birds will eat your flesh from you."

²⁰ On the third day it was Pharaoh's birthday, so he gave a feast for all his servants. He "lifted up" the head of the chief cupbearer and the head of the chief baker in the midst of his servants. ²¹ He restored the chief cupbearer to his former position so that he placed the cup in Pharaoh's hand, ²² but the chief baker he impaled, just as Joseph had predicted. ²³ But the chief cupbearer did not remember Joseph—he forgot him.

JOSEPH'S RISE TO POWER

41 At the end of two full years Pharaoh had a dream. As he was standing by the Nile, ² seven fine-looking, fat cows were coming up out of the Nile, and they grazed in the reeds. ³ Then seven bad-looking, thin cows were coming up after them from the Nile, and they stood beside the other cows at the edge of the river. ⁴ The bad-looking, thin cows ate the seven fine-looking, fat cows. Then Pharaoh woke up.

⁵ Then he fell asleep again and had a second dream: There were seven heads of grain growing on one stalk, healthy and good. ⁶ Then seven heads of grain, thin and burned by the east

CONTEMPLATE

Genesis 41:1–36

READ. Read the passage. Are there any verses or phrases that stand out? Consider the amount of time that passed before Pharaoh reached out to Joseph (v. 14), Joseph interpreted Pharaoh's dreams (vv. 25–32), or Joseph counseled Pharaoh (vv. 33–36).

MEDITATE. Meditate on God's timing and strategic placement of Joseph. How has God used you similarly to bring peace or wisdom to your sphere of influence? How can this story lead you to abide more deeply in the Person of Christ?

PRAY. Ask for discernment and wisdom in any situations you're facing. Pray that you will know and accept God's unique place and purpose for you.

CONTEMPLATE. If the weather allows, go for a walk or briefly step outside. Wherever you go, choose to enjoy the presence of your Creator.

wind, were sprouting up after them. ⁷ The thin heads swallowed up the seven healthy and full heads. Then Pharaoh woke up and realized it was a dream.

⁸ In the morning he was troubled, so he called for all the diviner-priests of Egypt and all its wise men. Pharaoh told them his dreams, but no one could interpret them for him. ⁹ Then the chief cupbearer said to Pharaoh, "Today I recall my failures. ¹⁰ Pharaoh was enraged with his servants, and he put me in prison in the house of the captain of the guards—me and the chief baker. ¹¹ We each had a dream one night; each of us had a dream with its own meaning. ¹² Now a young man, a Hebrew, a servant of the captain of the guards, was with us there. We told him our dreams, and he interpreted the meaning of each of our respective dreams for us. ¹³ It happened just as he had said to us—Pharaoh restored me to my office, but he impaled the baker."

¹⁴ Then Pharaoh summoned Joseph. So they brought him quickly out of the dungeon; he shaved himself, changed his clothes, and came before Pharaoh. ¹⁵ Pharaoh said to Joseph, "I had a dream, and there is no one who can interpret it. But I have heard about you, that you can interpret dreams." ¹⁶ Joseph replied to Pharaoh, "It is not within my power, but God will speak concerning the welfare of Pharaoh."

¹⁷ Then Pharaoh said to Joseph, "In my dream I was standing by the edge of the Nile. ¹⁸ Then seven fat and fine-looking cows were coming up out of the Nile, and they grazed in the reeds. ¹⁹ Then seven other cows came up after them; they were scrawny, very bad looking, and lean. I had never seen such bad-looking cows as these in all the land of Egypt! ²⁰ The lean, bad-looking cows ate up the seven fat cows. ²¹ When they had eaten them, no one would have known that they had done so, for they were just as bad-looking as before. Then I woke up. ²² I also saw in my dream seven heads of grain growing on one stalk, full and good. ²³ Then seven heads of grain, withered and thin and burned with the east wind, were sprouting up after them. ²⁴ The thin heads of grain swallowed up the seven good heads of grain. So I told all this to the diviner-priests, but no one could tell me its meaning."

²⁵ Then Joseph said to Pharaoh, "Both dreams of Pharaoh have the same meaning. God has revealed to Pharaoh what he is about to do. ²⁶ The seven good cows represent seven years, and the seven good heads of grain represent seven years. Both dreams have the same meaning. ²⁷ The seven lean, bad-looking cows that came up after them represent seven years, as do the seven empty heads of grain burned with the east wind. They represent seven years of famine. ²⁸ This is just what I told Pharaoh: God has shown Pharaoh what he is about to do. ²⁹ Seven years of great abundance are coming throughout the whole land of Egypt. ³⁰ But seven years of famine will occur after them, and all the abundance will be forgotten in the land of Egypt. The famine will devastate the land. ³¹ The previous abundance of the land will not be remembered because of the famine that follows, for the famine will be very severe. ³² The dream was repeated to Pharaoh because the matter has been decreed by God, and God will make it happen soon.

³³ "So now Pharaoh should look for a wise and discerning man and give him authority over all the land of Egypt. ³⁴ Pharaoh should do this—he should appoint officials throughout the land to collect one-fifth of the produce of the land of Egypt during the seven years of abundance. ³⁵ They should gather all the excess food during these good years that are coming. By Pharaoh's authority they should store up grain so the cities will have food, and they should preserve it. ³⁶ This food should be held in storage for the land in preparation for the seven years of famine that will occur throughout the land of Egypt. In this way the land will survive the famine."

³⁷ This advice made sense to Pharaoh and all his officials. ³⁸ So Pharaoh asked his officials, "Can we find a man like Joseph, one in whom the Spirit of God is present?" ³⁹ So Pharaoh said to Joseph, "Because God has enabled you to know all this, there is no one as wise and discerning as you are! ⁴⁰ You will oversee my household, and all my people will submit to your commands. Only I, the king, will be greater than you.

⁴¹ "See here," Pharaoh said to Joseph, "I place you in authority over all the land of Egypt." ⁴² Then Pharaoh took his signet ring from his own hand and put it on Joseph's. He clothed

PRAYING SCRIPTURE

Genesis 41:37–45

Focus your prayer on a careful reading of Genesis 41:38–40. Who in your life is a person in whom the Spirit of God resides? Notice that it was God who enabled Joseph to have wisdom and discernment. Thank God for the Spirit-filled person in your life. Pray that God would give you discernment and wisdom. For more about wisdom, see James 3:13–18.

Because God gave Joseph wisdom and favor, Pharaoh gave him increasing power and responsibility (v. 40). Pray that you would remain humble if God gives you promotions, power, or fame.

him with fine linen clothes and put a gold chain around his neck. ⁴³ Pharaoh had him ride in the chariot used by his second-in-command, and they cried out before him, "Kneel down!" So he placed him over all the land of Egypt. ⁴⁴ Pharaoh also said to Joseph, "I am Pharaoh, but without your permission no one will move his hand or his foot in all the land of Egypt." ⁴⁵ Pharaoh gave Joseph the name Zaphenath-Paneah. He also gave him Asenath daughter of Potiphera, priest of On, to be his wife. So Joseph took charge of all the land of Egypt.

⁴⁶ Now Joseph was 30 years old when he began serving Pharaoh king of Egypt. Joseph was commissioned by Pharaoh and was in charge of all the land of Egypt. ⁴⁷ During the seven years of abundance the land produced large, bountiful harvests. ⁴⁸ Joseph collected all the excess food in the land of Egypt during the seven years and stored it in the cities. In every city he put the food gathered from the fields around it. ⁴⁹ Joseph stored up a vast amount of grain, like the sand of the sea, until he stopped measuring it because it was impossible to measure.

⁵⁰ Two sons were born to Joseph before the famine came. Asenath daughter of Potiphera, priest of On, was their mother. ⁵¹ Joseph named the firstborn Manasseh, saying, "Certainly God has made me forget all my trouble and all my father's house." ⁵² He named the second child Ephraim, saying, "Certainly God has made me fruitful in the land of my suffering."

⁵³ The seven years of abundance in the land of Egypt came to an end. ⁵⁴ Then the seven years of famine began, just as Joseph had predicted. There was famine in all the other lands, but throughout the land of Egypt there was food. ⁵⁵ When all the land of Egypt experienced the famine, the people cried out to Pharaoh for food. Pharaoh said to all the people of Egypt, "Go to Joseph and do whatever he tells you."

⁵⁶ While the famine was over all the earth, Joseph opened the storehouses and sold grain to the Egyptians. The famine was severe throughout the land of Egypt. ⁵⁷ People from every country came to Joseph in Egypt to buy grain because the famine was severe throughout the earth.

JOSEPH'S BROTHERS IN EGYPT

42 When Jacob heard there was grain in Egypt, he said to his sons, "Why are you looking at each other?" [2] He then said, "Look, I hear that there is grain in Egypt. Go down there and buy grain for us so that we may live and not die."

[3] So ten of Joseph's brothers went down to buy grain from Egypt. [4] But Jacob did not send Joseph's brother Benjamin with his brothers, for he said, "What if some accident happens to him?" [5] So Israel's sons came to buy grain among the other travelers, for the famine was severe in the land of Canaan.

[6] Now Joseph was the ruler of the country, the one who sold grain to all the people of the country. Joseph's brothers came and bowed down before him with their faces to the ground. [7] When Joseph saw his brothers, he recognized them, but he pretended to be a stranger to them and spoke to them harshly. He asked, "Where do you come from?" They answered, "From the land of Canaan, to buy grain for food."

[8] Joseph recognized his brothers, but they did not recognize him. [9] Then Joseph remembered the dreams he had dreamed about them, and he said to them, "You are spies; you have come to see if our land is vulnerable!"

[10] But they exclaimed, "No, my lord! Your servants have come to buy grain for food! [11] We are all the sons of one man; we are honest men! Your servants are not spies."

[12] "No," he insisted, "but you have come to see if our land is vulnerable." [13] They replied, "Your servants are from a family of twelve brothers. We are the sons of one man in the land of Canaan. The youngest is with our father at this time, and one is no longer alive."

[14] But Joseph told them, "It is just as I said to you: You are spies! [15] You will be tested in this way: As surely as Pharaoh lives, you will not depart from this place unless your youngest brother comes here. [16] One of you must go and get your brother, while the rest of you remain in prison. In this way your words may be tested to see if you are telling the truth. If not, then, as surely as Pharaoh lives, you are spies!" [17] He imprisoned them all for three days. [18] On the third day Joseph said to them, "Do as I say and you will live, for I fear God. [19] If

CONTEMPLATE

Genesis 42:1–11

READ. Read the passage and imagine its details. Locate a verse that stands out to you. Consider the significance of the moment in verse 6 or Joseph's response in verse 7. Meditate on the verse and its meaning within context.

MEDITATE. How are God's sovereignty and rule demonstrated throughout the course of Joseph's life? Why might Joseph have chosen to conceal his identity?

PRAY. Ask the Holy Spirit to empower you to extend love and forgiveness to any family members who may have wronged you.

CONTEMPLATE. After praying, consider the cross. Christ was rejected and despised by the very ones He came to save. Yet the Lord longs to be gracious, and He rises to show mercy at the sound of a repentant cry (Isa 30:18–19). Be willing to forgive and extend mercy.

 JOURNAL

Genesis 42:18–24

REFLECT AND WRITE.

- How did the brothers feel when Joseph gave his directions? How did Joseph feel when he overheard his brothers' conversation?

- What can you learn about God's nature and character through this story? Find similar traits of God in other passages of Scripture.

you are honest men, leave one of your brothers confined here in prison while the rest of you go and take grain back for your hungry families. ²⁰ But you must bring your youngest brother to me. Then your words will be verified and you will not die." They did as he said.

²¹ They said to one another, "Surely we're being punished because of our brother, because we saw how distressed he was when he cried to us for mercy, but we refused to listen. That is why this distress has come on us!" ²² Reuben said to them, "Didn't I say to you, 'Don't sin against the boy,' but you wouldn't listen? So now we must pay for shedding his blood!" ²³ (Now they did not know that Joseph could understand them, for he was speaking through an interpreter.) ²⁴ He turned away from them and wept. When he turned around and spoke to them again, he had Simeon taken from them and tied up before their eyes.

²⁵ Then Joseph gave orders to fill their bags with grain, to return each man's money to his sack, and to give them provisions for the journey. His orders were carried out. ²⁶ So they loaded their grain on their donkeys and left.

²⁷ When one of them opened his sack to get feed for his donkey at their resting place, he saw his money in the mouth of his sack. ²⁸ He said to his brothers, "My money was returned! Here it is in my sack!" They were dismayed; they turned trembling to one another and said, "What in the world has God done to us?"

²⁹ They returned to their father Jacob in the land of Canaan and told him all the things that had happened to them, saying, ³⁰ "The man, the lord of the land, spoke harshly to us and treated us as if we were spying on the land. ³¹ But we said to him, 'We are honest men; we are not spies! ³² We are from a family of twelve brothers; we are the sons of one father. One is no longer alive, and the youngest is with our father at this time in the land of Canaan.'

³³ "Then the man, the lord of the land, said to us, 'This is how I will find out if you are honest men. Leave one of your brothers with me, and take grain for your hungry households and go. ³⁴ But bring your youngest brother back to me so I will

CONTEMPLATE

Genesis 42:25–38

READ. Read the passage twice, meditating especially on verse 28 or verse 38 for meaning and context. Pay attention to what the Spirit might teach you.

MEDITATE. Reflect on the emotions that Joseph's father and brothers must have felt in these situations. You may not have experienced these same circumstances, but have you experienced similar emotions? Have you taken that experience to God?

PRAY. Pray that this passage will assure you that God neither forgets nor forsakes a grieving parent. Pray that you will wait on God and abide in Christ in all matters of the heart.

CONTEMPLATE. Take a moment to be silent in God's presence. Rest in His sovereignty, and place your trust in your loving Father's heart.

know that you are honest men and not spies. Then I will give your brother back to you and you may move about freely in the land.'"

35 When they were emptying their sacks, there was each man's bag of money in his sack! When they and their father saw the bags of money, they were afraid. 36 Their father Jacob said to them, "You are making me childless! Joseph is gone. Simeon is gone. And now you want to take Benjamin! Everything is against me."

37 Then Reuben said to his father, "You may put my two sons to death if I do not bring him back to you. Put him in my care and I will bring him back to you." 38 But Jacob replied, "My son will not go down there with you, for his brother is dead and he alone is left. If an accident happens to him on the journey you have to make, then you will bring down my gray hair in sorrow to the grave."

THE SECOND JOURNEY TO EGYPT

43 Now the famine was severe in the land. 2 When they finished eating the grain they had brought from Egypt, their father said to them, "Return, buy us a little more food."

3 But Judah said to him, "The man solemnly warned us, 'You will not see my face unless your brother is with you.' 4 If you send our brother with us, we'll go down and buy food for you. 5 But if you will not send him, we won't go down there because the man said to us, 'You will not see my face unless your brother is with you.'"

6 Israel said, "Why did you bring this trouble on me by telling the man you had one more brother?"

7 They replied, "The man questioned us thoroughly about ourselves and our family, saying, 'Is your father still alive? Do you have another brother?' So we answered him in this way. How could we possibly know that he would say, 'Bring your brother down'?"

8 Then Judah said to his father Israel, "Send the boy with me and we will go immediately. Then we will live and not die—we and you and our little ones. 9 I myself pledge security

JOURNAL

Genesis 43:8–17

REFLECT AND WRITE.

- What assurances did Judah give his father regarding Benjamin's safety? What do you think were Israel's true feelings about the plan?

- Compare Joseph's reaction to seeing his brothers (see vv. 15–17) with the father's reaction to his son's return in the parable of the compassionate father (see Luke 15:11–24). How does Joseph's reaction demonstrate God's heart for His people?

for him; you may hold me liable. If I do not bring him back to you and place him here before you, I will bear the blame before you all my life. ¹⁰ But if we had not delayed, we could have traveled there and back twice by now!"

¹¹ Then their father Israel said to them, "If it must be so, then do this: Take some of the best products of the land in your bags, and take a gift down to the man—a little balm and a little honey, spices and myrrh, pistachios and almonds. ¹² Take double the money with you; you must take back the money that was returned in the mouths of your sacks—perhaps it was an oversight. ¹³ Take your brother too, and go right away to the man. ¹⁴ May the Sovereign God grant you mercy before the man so that he may release your other brother and Benjamin! As for me, if I lose my children I lose them."

¹⁵ So the men took these gifts, and they took double the money with them, along with Benjamin. Then they hurried down to Egypt and stood before Joseph. ¹⁶ When Joseph saw Benjamin with them, he said to the servant who was over his household, "Bring the men to the house. Slaughter an animal and prepare it, for the men will eat with me at noon." ¹⁷ The man did just as Joseph said; he brought the men into Joseph's house.

¹⁸ But the men were afraid when they were brought to Joseph's house. They said, "We are being brought in because of the money that was returned in our sacks last time. He wants to capture us, make us slaves, and take our donkeys!" ¹⁹ So they approached the man who was in charge of Joseph's household and spoke to him at the entrance to the house. ²⁰ They said, "My lord, we did indeed come down the first time to buy food. ²¹ But when we came to the place where we spent the night, we opened our sacks and each of us found his money—the full amount—in the mouth of his sack. So we have returned it. ²² We have brought additional money with us to buy food. We do not know who put the money in our sacks!"

²³ "Everything is fine," the man in charge of Joseph's household told them. "Don't be afraid. Your God and the God of your father has given you treasure in your sacks. I had your money." Then he brought Simeon out to them.

PRAYING
SCRIPTURE

Genesis 43:18–34

After many years, Joseph met his brothers who had sold him into slavery. Meditate on what that situation must have been like for Joseph. Anger, love, pain, confusion—these emotions and more must have churned within Joseph's soul (v. 30). If you had been Joseph, what would you have done? Pray that God would help you bring peace to difficult relationships. Pray for peace in your own heart (John 14:27).

²⁴The servant in charge brought the men into Joseph's house. He gave them water, and they washed their feet. Then he gave food to their donkeys. ²⁵They got their gifts ready for Joseph's arrival at noon, for they had heard that they were to have a meal there.

²⁶When Joseph came home, they presented him with the gifts they had brought inside, and they bowed down to the ground before him. ²⁷He asked them how they were doing. Then he said, "Is your aging father well, the one you spoke about? Is he still alive?" ²⁸"Your servant our father is well," they replied. "He is still alive." They bowed down in humility.

²⁹When Joseph looked up and saw his brother Benjamin, his mother's son, he said, "Is this your youngest brother, whom you told me about?" Then he said, "May God be gracious to you, my son." ³⁰Joseph hurried out, for he was overcome by affection for his brother and was at the point of tears. So he went to his room and wept there.

³¹Then he washed his face and came out. With composure he said, "Set out the food." ³²They set a place for him, a separate place for his brothers, and another for the Egyptians who were eating with him. (The Egyptians are not able to eat with Hebrews, for the Egyptians think it is disgusting to do so.) ³³They sat before him, arranged by order of birth, beginning with the firstborn and ending with the youngest. The men looked at each other in astonishment. ³⁴He gave them portions of the food set before him, but the portion for Benjamin was five times greater than the portions for any of the others. They drank with Joseph until they all became drunk.

THE FINAL TEST

44 He instructed the servant who was over his household, "Fill the sacks of the men with as much food as they can carry and put each man's money in the mouth of his sack. ²Then put my cup—the silver cup—in the mouth of the youngest one's sack, along with the money for his grain." He did as Joseph instructed.

JOURNAL

Genesis 44:1–14

REFLECT AND WRITE.

- Why do you think Joseph hadn't yet revealed himself to his brothers?

- Reflect on the older brothers' response to the cup being found in Benjamin's sack. What was Joseph's purpose in having his cup planted in his younger brother's bag?

- How did verse 14 fulfill Joseph's dream back in Genesis 37:7–10?

³ When morning came, the men and their donkeys were sent off. ⁴ They had not gone very far from the city when Joseph said to the servant who was over his household, "Pursue the men at once! When you overtake them, say to them, 'Why have you repaid good with evil? ⁵ Doesn't my master drink from this cup and use it for divination? You have done wrong!'"

⁶ When the man overtook them, he spoke these words to them. ⁷ They answered him, "Why does my lord say such things? Far be it from your servants to do such a thing! ⁸ Look, the money that we found in the mouths of our sacks we brought back to you from the land of Canaan. Why then would we steal silver or gold from your master's house? ⁹ If one of us has it, he will die, and the rest of us will become my lord's slaves!"

¹⁰ He replied, "You have suggested your own punishment! The one who has it will become my slave, but the rest of you will go free." ¹¹ So each man quickly lowered his sack to the ground and opened it. ¹² Then the man searched. He began with the oldest and finished with the youngest. The cup was found in Benjamin's sack! ¹³ They all tore their clothes! Then each man loaded his donkey, and they returned to the city.

¹⁴ So Judah and his brothers came back to Joseph's house. He was still there, and they threw themselves to the ground before him. ¹⁵ Joseph said to them, "What did you think you were doing? Don't you know that a man like me can find out things like this by divination?"

¹⁶ Judah replied, "What can we say to my lord? What can we speak? How can we clear ourselves? God has exposed the sin of your servants! We are now my lord's slaves, we and the one in whose possession the cup was found."

¹⁷ But Joseph said, "Far be it from me to do this! The man in whose hand the cup was found will become my slave, but the rest of you may go back to your father in peace."

¹⁸ Then Judah approached him and said, "My lord, please allow your servant to speak a word with you. Please do not get angry with your servant, for you are just like Pharaoh. ¹⁹ My lord asked his servants, 'Do you have a father or a brother?' ²⁰ We said to my lord, 'We have an aged father, and there is a young boy who was born when our father was old. The boy's

PRAYING
SCRIPTURE

Genesis 44:18–34

As you read Judah's account of the events, what emotions or thoughts come to mind? Judah, along with his brothers, had previously sold Joseph into slavery and then falsely told his father that Joseph was dead. Now Judah demonstrated humility by showing great concern for his father and his brother Benjamin (vv. 33–34). He even offered to trade places with Benjamin. Do you think God changed Judah's heart over the years? Pray that God would help you continually become more and more like Christ.

brother is dead. He is the only one of his mother's sons left, and his father loves him.'

21 "Then you told your servants, 'Bring him down to me so I can see him.' 22 We said to my lord, 'The boy cannot leave his father. If he leaves his father, his father will die.' 23 But you said to your servants, 'If your youngest brother does not come down with you, you will not see my face again.' 24 When we returned to your servant my father, we told him the words of my lord.

25 "Then our father said, 'Go back and buy us a little food.' 26 But we replied, 'We cannot go down there. If our youngest brother is with us, then we will go, for we won't be permitted to see the man's face if our youngest brother is not with us.'

27 "Then your servant my father said to us, 'You know that my wife gave me two sons. 28 The first disappeared and I said, "He has surely been torn to pieces." I have not seen him since. 29 If you take this one from me too and an accident happens to him, then you will bring down my gray hair in tragedy to the grave.'

30 "So now, when I return to your servant my father, and the boy is not with us—his very life is bound up in his son's life. 31 When he sees the boy is not with us, he will die, and your servants will bring down the gray hair of your servant our father in sorrow to the grave. 32 Indeed, your servant pledged security for the boy with my father, saying, 'If I do not bring him back to you, then I will bear the blame before my father all my life.'

33 "So now, please let your servant remain as my lord's slave instead of the boy. As for the boy, let him go back with his brothers. 34 For how can I go back to my father if the boy is not with me? I couldn't bear to see my father's pain."

THE RECONCILIATION OF THE BROTHERS

45 Joseph was no longer able to control himself before all his attendants, so he cried out, "Make everyone go out from my presence!" No one remained with Joseph when he made himself known to his brothers. 2 He wept loudly; the Egyptians heard it and Pharaoh's household heard about it.

CONTEMPLATE

Genesis 45:1–8

READ. Ask God to reveal Himself to you through His Word. Then read the passage twice. Choose a verse to meditate on. Consider verse 5, 7, or 8.

MEDITATE. How does this verse speak to you? Have you or someone close to you been thrown into circumstances you did not deserve? Have you witnessed God use the trial to bless other people (see Gen 50:20)? What does this verse tell you about God's character and His providence?

PRAY. Ask for eyes to see God at work around you. Pray for perseverance through suffering or tribulation, knowing that these things bring about character and hope (Rom 5:3–5).

CONTEMPLATE. Read Romans 5:3–5 along with James 1:2–4. Resolve to live a life of perseverance and of trust in God's wisdom and plans.

³Joseph said to his brothers, "I am Joseph! Is my father still alive?" His brothers could not answer him because they were dumbfounded before him. ⁴Joseph said to his brothers, "Come closer to me," so they came near. Then he said, "I am Joseph your brother, whom you sold into Egypt. ⁵Now, do not be upset and do not be angry with yourselves because you sold me here, for God sent me ahead of you to preserve life! ⁶For these past two years there has been famine in the land and for five more years there will be neither plowing nor harvesting. ⁷God sent me ahead of you to preserve you on the earth and to save your lives by a great deliverance. ⁸So now, it is not you who sent me here, but God. He has made me an adviser to Pharaoh, lord over all his household, and ruler over all the land of Egypt. ⁹Now go up to my father quickly and tell him, 'This is what your son Joseph says: "God has made me lord of all Egypt. Come down to me; do not delay! ¹⁰You will live in the land of Goshen, and you will be near me—you, your children, your grandchildren, your flocks, your herds, and everything you have. ¹¹I will provide you with food there because there will be five more years of famine. Otherwise you would become poor—you, your household, and everyone who belongs to you.'" ¹²You and my brother Benjamin can certainly see with your own eyes that I really am the one who speaks to you. ¹³So tell my father about all my honor in Egypt and about everything you have seen. But bring my father down here quickly!"

¹⁴Then he threw himself on the neck of his brother Benjamin and wept, and Benjamin wept on his neck. ¹⁵He kissed all his brothers and wept over them. After this his brothers talked with him.

¹⁶Now it was reported in the household of Pharaoh, "Joseph's brothers have arrived." It pleased Pharaoh and his servants. ¹⁷Pharaoh said to Joseph, "Say to your brothers, 'Do this: Load your animals and go to the land of Canaan! ¹⁸Get your father and your households and come to me! Then I will give you the best land in Egypt and you will eat the best of the land.' ¹⁹You are also commanded to say, 'Do this: Take for yourselves wagons from the land of Egypt for your little ones and for your wives. Bring your father and come. ²⁰Don't

JOURNAL

Genesis 45:9–28

REFLECT AND WRITE.

- What do you think Joseph's brothers were feeling? What emotions would Jacob have experienced upon hearing about Joseph? What feelings must Joseph have experienced when he revealed himself to his brothers?

- How did Joseph provide for his family in their time of need? How did this demonstrate God's provision for His people? How can this knowledge lead you to a deeper relationship with the God who provides (see Gen 22:14)?

worry about your belongings, for the best of all the land of Egypt will be yours.'"

21 So the sons of Israel did as he said. Joseph gave them wagons as Pharaoh had instructed, and he gave them provisions for the journey. 22 He gave sets of clothes to each one of them, but to Benjamin he gave 300 pieces of silver and five sets of clothes. 23 To his father he sent the following: ten donkeys loaded with the best products of Egypt and ten female donkeys loaded with grain, food, and provisions for his father's journey. 24 Then he sent his brothers on their way and they left. He said to them, "As you travel don't be overcome with fear."

25 So they went up from Egypt and came to their father Jacob in the land of Canaan. 26 They told him, "Joseph is still alive and he is ruler over all the land of Egypt!" Jacob was stunned, for he did not believe them. 27 But when they related to him everything Joseph had said to them, and when he saw the wagons that Joseph had sent to transport him, their father Jacob's spirit revived. 28 Then Israel said, "Enough! My son Joseph is still alive! I will go and see him before I die."

THE FAMILY OF JACOB GOES TO EGYPT

46 So Israel began his journey, taking with him all that he had. When he came to Beer Sheba he offered sacrifices to the God of his father Isaac. 2 God spoke to Israel in a vision during the night and said, "Jacob, Jacob!" He replied, "Here I am!" 3 He said, "I am God, the God of your father. Do not be afraid to go down to Egypt, for I will make you into a great nation there. 4 I will go down with you to Egypt and I myself will certainly bring you back from there. Joseph will close your eyes."

5 Then Jacob started out from Beer Sheba, and the sons of Israel carried their father Jacob, their little children, and their wives in the wagons that Pharaoh had sent along to transport him. 6 Jacob and all his descendants took their livestock and the possessions they had acquired in the land of Canaan, and they went to Egypt. 7 He brought with him to Egypt his

PRAYING
SCRIPTURE

Genesis 46:1–4

Jacob, now quite old, received a vision from God on the way to Egypt. God told him to not be afraid of entering this foreign land. God affirmed that He would make Jacob a great nation in Egypt, where his son Joseph was a high-level political leader. God finally showed Jacob the larger purpose of Joseph's painful story.

How does God's revelation to Jacob help you go through uncertain, difficult times? Ask God to help you trust Him in all things. How have you seen God's faithful hand in your journey?

sons and grandsons, his daughters and granddaughters—all his descendants.

8 These are the names of the sons of Israel who went to Egypt—Jacob and his sons: Reuben, the firstborn of Jacob.

9 The sons of Reuben: Hanoch, Pallu, Hezron, and Carmi.

10 The sons of Simeon: Jemuel, Jamin, Ohad, Jakin, Zohar, and Shaul (the son of a Canaanite woman).

11 The sons of Levi: Gershon, Kohath, and Merari.

12 The sons of Judah: Er, Onan, Shelah, Perez, and Zerah (but Er and Onan died in the land of Canaan). The sons of Perez were Hezron and Hamul.

13 The sons of Issachar: Tola, Puah, Jashub, and Shimron.

14 The sons of Zebulun: Sered, Elon, and Jahleel.

15 These were the sons of Leah, whom she bore to Jacob in Paddan Aram, along with Dinah his daughter. His sons and daughters numbered thirty-three in all.

16 The sons of Gad: Zephon, Haggi, Shuni, Ezbon, Eri, Arodi, and Areli.

17 The sons of Asher: Imnah, Ishvah, Ishvi, Beriah, and Serah their sister. The sons of Beriah were Heber and Malkiel.

18 These were the sons of Zilpah, whom Laban gave to Leah his daughter. She bore these to Jacob, sixteen in all.

19 The sons of Rachel the wife of Jacob: Joseph and Benjamin.

20 Manasseh and Ephraim were born to Joseph in the land of Egypt. Asenath daughter of Potiphera, priest of On, bore them to him.

21 The sons of Benjamin: Bela, Beker, Ashbel, Gera, Naaman, Ehi, Rosh, Muppim, Huppim and Ard.

22 These were the sons of Rachel who were born to Jacob, fourteen in all.

23 The son of Dan: Hushim.

24 The sons of Naphtali: Jahziel, Guni, Jezer, and Shillem.

25 These were the sons of Bilhah, whom Laban gave to Rachel his daughter. She bore these to Jacob, seven in all.

²⁶ All the direct descendants of Jacob who went to Egypt with him were sixty-six in number. (This number does not include the wives of Jacob's sons.) ²⁷ Counting the two sons of Joseph who were born to him in Egypt, all the people of the household of Jacob who were in Egypt numbered seventy.

²⁸ Jacob sent Judah before him to Joseph to accompany him to Goshen. So they came to the land of Goshen. ²⁹ Joseph harnessed his chariot and went up to meet his father Israel in Goshen. When he met him, he hugged his neck and wept on his neck for quite some time.

³⁰ Israel said to Joseph, "Now let me die since I have seen your face and know that you are still alive." ³¹ Then Joseph said to his brothers and his father's household, "I will go up and tell Pharaoh, 'My brothers and my father's household who were in the land of Canaan have come to me. ³² The men are shepherds; they take care of livestock. They have brought their flocks and their herds and all that they have.' ³³ Pharaoh will summon you and say, 'What is your occupation?' ³⁴ Tell him, 'Your servants have taken care of cattle from our youth until now, both we and our fathers,' so that you may live in the land of Goshen, for everyone who takes care of sheep is disgusting to the Egyptians."

JOSEPH'S WISE ADMINISTRATION

47 Joseph went and told Pharaoh, "My father, my brothers, their flocks and herds, and all that they own have arrived from the land of Canaan. They are now in the land of Goshen." ² He took five of his brothers and introduced them to Pharaoh.

³ Pharaoh said to Joseph's brothers, "What is your occupation?" They said to Pharaoh, "Your servants take care of flocks, just as our ancestors did." ⁴ Then they said to Pharaoh, "We have come to live as temporary residents in the land. There is no pasture for your servants' flocks because the famine is severe in the land of Canaan. So now, please let your servants live in the land of Goshen."

⁵ Pharaoh said to Joseph, "Your father and your brothers have come to you. ⁶ The land of Egypt is before you; settle your

CONTEMPLATE

Genesis 47:1–6

READ. Review Genesis 46:34. Then read Genesis 47:1–6 twice. Choose a phrase to meditate on: "Your servants take care of flocks" (v. 3) or "Settle your father and your brothers in the best region of the land" (v. 6). Meditate on the phrase for meaning and context.

MEDITATE. Has God ever shown you favor among unbelievers or others who otherwise might despise you? Did you receive even a portion of their best? Couple this meditation with Psalm 23.

PRAY. Thank Jesus that He is the good shepherd who gave His life for the sheep (John 10:11). Praise Him that He knows you and you hear His voice (John 10:27). Ask Him to draw you closer to Him as He watches over the fold.

CONTEMPLATE. Rest in the presence of the Lord who restores your soul.

father and your brothers in the best region of the land. They may live in the land of Goshen. If you know of any highly capable men among them, put them in charge of my livestock."

⁷ Then Joseph brought in his father Jacob and presented him before Pharaoh. Jacob blessed Pharaoh. ⁸ Pharaoh said to Jacob, "How long have you lived?" ⁹ Jacob said to Pharaoh, "All the years of my travels are 130. All the years of my life have been few and painful; the years of my travels are not as long as those of my ancestors." ¹⁰ Then Jacob blessed Pharaoh and went out from his presence.

¹¹ So Joseph settled his father and his brothers. He gave them territory in the land of Egypt, in the best region of the land, the land of Rameses, just as Pharaoh had commanded. ¹² Joseph also provided food for his father, his brothers, and all his father's household, according to the number of their little children.

¹³ But there was no food in all the land because the famine was very severe; the land of Egypt and the land of Canaan wasted away because of the famine. ¹⁴ Joseph collected all the money that could be found in the land of Egypt and in the land of Canaan as payment for the grain they were buying. Then Joseph brought the money into Pharaoh's palace. ¹⁵ When the money from the lands of Egypt and Canaan was used up, all the Egyptians came to Joseph and said, "Give us food! Why should we die before your very eyes because our money has run out?"

¹⁶ Then Joseph said, "If your money is gone, bring your livestock, and I will give you food in exchange for your livestock." ¹⁷ So they brought their livestock to Joseph, and Joseph gave them food in exchange for their horses, the livestock of their flocks and herds, and their donkeys. He got them through that year by giving them food in exchange for all their livestock.

¹⁸ When that year was over, they came to him the next year and said to him, "We cannot hide from our lord that the money is used up and the livestock and the animals belong to our lord. Nothing remains before our lord except our bodies and our land. ¹⁹ Why should we die before your very eyes, both we and our land? Buy us and our land in exchange

JOURNAL

Genesis 47:16–24

REFLECT AND WRITE.

- How did Joseph show great leadership during the famine? Do you think he was wise to eventually obtain all that the Egyptians owned in exchange for food?

- How was Joseph a blessing to the people in their time of need? Can you give examples of how God has blessed you in your time of need?

for food, and we, with our land, will become Pharaoh's slaves. Give us seed that we may live and not die. Then the land will not become desolate."

20 So Joseph bought all the land of Egypt for Pharaoh. Each of the Egyptians sold his field, for the famine was severe. So the land became Pharaoh's. 21 Joseph made all the people slaves from one end of Egypt's border to the other end of it. 22 But he did not purchase the land of the priests because the priests had an allotment from Pharaoh and they ate from their allotment that Pharaoh gave them. That is why they did not sell their land.

23 Joseph said to the people, "Since I have bought you and your land today for Pharaoh, here is seed for you. Cultivate the land. 24 When the crop comes in, give one-fifth of it to Pharaoh. The remaining four-fifths will be yours for seed for the fields and for you to eat, including those in your households and your little children." 25 They replied, "You have saved our lives! You are showing us favor, and we will be Pharaoh's slaves."

26 So Joseph made it a statute, which is in effect to this day throughout the land of Egypt: One-fifth belongs to Pharaoh. Only the land of the priests did not become Pharaoh's.

27 Israel settled in the land of Egypt, in the land of Goshen, and they owned land there. They were fruitful and increased rapidly in number.

28 Jacob lived in the land of Egypt seventeen years; the years of Jacob's life were 147 in all. 29 The time for Israel to die approached, so he called for his son Joseph and said to him, "If now I have found favor in your sight, put your hand under my thigh and show me kindness and faithfulness. Do not bury me in Egypt, 30 but when I rest with my fathers, carry me out of Egypt and bury me in their burial place." Joseph said, "I will do as you say."

31 Jacob said, "Swear to me that you will do so." So Joseph gave him his word. Then Israel bowed down at the head of his bed.

MANASSEH AND EPHRAIM

48 After these things Joseph was told, "Your father is weakening." So he took his two sons Manasseh and Ephraim with him. ² When Jacob was told, "Your son Joseph has just come to you," Israel regained strength and sat up on his bed. ³ Jacob said to Joseph, "The Sovereign God appeared to me at Luz in the land of Canaan and blessed me. ⁴ He said to me, 'I am going to make you fruitful and will multiply you. I will make you into a group of nations, and I will give this land to your descendants as an everlasting possession.'

⁵ "Now, as for your two sons, who were born to you in the land of Egypt before I came to you in Egypt, they will be mine. Ephraim and Manasseh will be mine just as Reuben and Simeon are. ⁶ Any children that you father after them will be yours; they will be listed under the names of their brothers in their inheritance. ⁷ But as for me, when I was returning from Paddan, Rachel died—to my sorrow—in the land of Canaan. It happened along the way, some distance from Ephrath. So I buried her there on the way to Ephrath" (that is, Bethlehem).

⁸ When Israel saw Joseph's sons, he asked, "Who are these?" ⁹ Joseph said to his father, "They are the sons God has given me in this place." His father said, "Bring them to me so I may bless them." ¹⁰ Now Israel's eyes were failing because of his age; he was not able to see well. So Joseph brought his sons near to him, and his father kissed them and embraced them. ¹¹ Israel said to Joseph, "I never expected to see you again, but now God has allowed me to see your children too."

¹² So Joseph moved them from Israel's knees and bowed down with his face to the ground. ¹³ Joseph positioned them; he put Ephraim on his right hand across from Israel's left hand, and Manasseh on his left hand across from Israel's right hand. Then Joseph brought them closer to his father. ¹⁴ Israel stretched out his right hand and placed it on Ephraim's head, although he was the younger. Crossing his hands, he put his left hand on Manasseh's head, for Manasseh was the firstborn.

JOURNAL

Genesis 48:10–20

REFLECT AND WRITE.

- Where else in the Bible did the firstborn fail to receive the blessing (see, for example, Gen 17:18–21; 27:19–41; 1 Chr 5:1–2)? Why was a blessing such a big deal?

- How does the way Jacob switched the blessings for Joseph's sons demonstrate the sovereignty of God and His plans for humanity?

¹⁵ Then he blessed Joseph and said,
"May the God before whom my fathers
Abraham and Isaac walked—
the God who has been my shepherd
all my life long to this day,
¹⁶   the angel who has protected me
from all harm—
bless these boys.
May my name be named in them,
and the name of my fathers Abraham and Isaac.
May they grow into a multitude on the earth."

¹⁷ When Joseph saw that his father placed his right hand on Ephraim's head, it displeased him. So he took his father's hand to move it from Ephraim's head to Manasseh's head. ¹⁸ Joseph said to his father, "Not so, my father, for this is the firstborn. Put your right hand on his head." ¹⁹ But his father refused and said, "I know, my son, I know. He too will become a nation and he too will become great. In spite of this, his younger brother will be even greater and his descendants will become a multitude of nations." ²⁰ So he blessed them that day, saying,
"By you will Israel bless, saying,
'May God make you like Ephraim and Manasseh.'"
Thus he put Ephraim before Manasseh.

²¹ Then Israel said to Joseph, "I am about to die, but God will be with you and will bring you back to the land of your fathers. ²² As one who is above your brothers, I give to you the mountain slope, which I took from the Amorites with my sword and my bow."

THE BLESSING OF JACOB

49 Jacob called for his sons and said, "Gather together so I can tell you what will happen to you in future days.
²   "Assemble and listen, you sons of Jacob;
listen to Israel, your father.

3 Reuben, you are my firstborn,
my might and the beginning of my strength,
outstanding in dignity, outstanding in power.

4 You are destructive like water and will not excel,
for you got on your father's bed,
then you defiled it—he got on my couch!

5 Simeon and Levi are brothers,
weapons of violence are their knives!

6 O my soul, do not come into their council,
do not be united to their assembly, my heart,
for in their anger they have killed men,
and for pleasure they have hamstrung oxen.

7 Cursed be their anger, for it was fierce,
and their fury, for it was cruel.
I will divide them in Jacob,
and scatter them in Israel!

8 Judah, your brothers will praise you.
Your hand will be on the neck of your enemies,
your father's sons will bow down before you.

9 You are a lion's cub, Judah,
from the prey, my son, you have gone up.
He crouches and lies down like a lion;
like a lioness—who will rouse him?

10 The scepter will not depart from Judah,
nor the ruler's staff from between his feet,
until he comes to whom it belongs;
the nations will obey him.

11 Binding his foal to the vine,
and his colt to the choicest vine,
he will wash his garments in wine,
his robes in the blood of grapes.

12 His eyes will be red from wine,
and his teeth white from milk.

13 Zebulun will live by the haven of the sea
and become a haven for ships;
his border will extend to Sidon.

14 Issachar is a strong-boned donkey
lying down between two saddlebags.

PRAYING SCRIPTURE

Genesis 49:8–12

As Jacob neared death, he blessed his sons. Jacob gave leadership to Judah, even though he was the fourth child. Has God bestowed leadership on you, even at a small level? Pray that God will help you be faithful with that responsibility.

Jesus, a descendant of Judah, was later referred to as the "Lion of the tribe of Judah" (Rev 5:5). Since Jacob's time, God has been gradually revealing His plan of salvation through Jesus. Christ fulfilled this prophecy (v. 10). Meditate on our awesome God who works out His plans through the generations.

15   When he sees a good resting place,
and the pleasant land,
he will bend his shoulder to the burden
and become a slave laborer.

16   Dan will judge his people
as one of the tribes of Israel.

17   May Dan be a snake beside the road,
a viper by the path,
that bites the heels of the horse
so that its rider falls backward.

18   I wait for your deliverance, O LORD.

19   Gad will be raided by marauding bands,
but he will attack them at their heels.

20   Asher's food will be rich,
and he will provide delicacies to royalty.

21   Naphtali is a free running doe,
he speaks delightful words.

22   Joseph is a fruitful bough,
a fruitful bough near a spring
whose branches climb over the wall.

23   The archers will attack him,
they will shoot at him and oppose him.

24   But his bow will remain steady,
and his hands will be skillful;
because of the hands of the Powerful One of Jacob,
because of the Shepherd, the Rock of Israel,

25   because of the God of your father,
who will help you,
because of the Sovereign God,
who will bless you
with blessings from the sky above,
blessings from the deep that lies below,
and blessings of the breasts and womb.

26   The blessings of your father are greater
than the blessings of the eternal mountains
or the desirable things of the age-old hills.
They will be on the head of Joseph
and on the brow of the prince of his brothers.

CONTEMPLATE

Genesis 49:22–26

READ. Read the passage and choose a word or phrase to meditate on. Perhaps it is "fruitful" (v. 22) or "blessings" (vv. 25–26).

MEDITATE. How was Joseph fruitful and blessed? How are you fruitful and blessed? How have you responded to God for His kindness to you in the past? How does Jacob's blessing for his son Joseph draw you closer to the Father's heart? How will you allow it to strengthen your bond with Christ?

PRAY. Praise God for the many blessings He has bestowed on your life. Praise Him for specific blessings. Then ask the Spirit to bring more to mind. Ask God to increase the fruit of your life's ministry for His glory.

CONTEMPLATE. Practice a quiet moment of gratitude with the Lord.

27   Benjamin is a ravenous wolf;
     in the morning devouring the prey,
     and in the evening dividing the plunder."

²⁸ These are the twelve tribes of Israel. This is what their father said to them when he blessed them. He gave each of them an appropriate blessing.

²⁹ Then he instructed them, "I am about to go to my people. Bury me with my fathers in the cave in the field of Ephron the Hittite. ³⁰ It is the cave in the field of Machpelah, near Mamre in the land of Canaan, which Abraham bought for a burial plot from Ephron the Hittite. ³¹ There they buried Abraham and his wife Sarah; there they buried Isaac and his wife Rebekah; and there I buried Leah. ³² The field and the cave in it were acquired from the sons of Heth."

³³ When Jacob finished giving these instructions to his sons, he pulled his feet up onto the bed, breathed his last breath, and went to his people.

THE BURIALS OF JACOB AND JOSEPH

50 Then Joseph hugged his father's face. He wept over him and kissed him. ² Joseph instructed the physicians in his service to embalm his father, so the physicians embalmed Israel. ³ They took forty days, for that is the full time needed for embalming. The Egyptians mourned for him seventy days.

⁴ When the days of mourning had passed, Joseph said to Pharaoh's royal court, "If I have found favor in your sight, please say to Pharaoh, ⁵ 'My father made me swear an oath. He said, "I am about to die. Bury me in my tomb that I dug for myself there in the land of Canaan." Now let me go and bury my father; then I will return.'" ⁶ So Pharaoh said, "Go and bury your father, just as he made you swear to do."

⁷ So Joseph went up to bury his father; all Pharaoh's officials went with him—the senior courtiers of his household, all the senior officials of the land of Egypt, ⁸ all Joseph's household, his brothers, and his father's household. But they left their little children and their flocks and herds in the land of

JOURNAL

Genesis 49:29–33

REFLECT AND WRITE.

- Why did Jacob insist on being buried with his ancestors in the land of Canaan rather than in Goshen?

- What aspects of Jacob's story and life (see Gen 25–35, 46–49) lead you to worship God? Bring any questions you still have regarding Jacob's story before God now. How does Jacob's life influence how you live your life for Christ?

PRAYING SCRIPTURE

Genesis 50:1–6

What love Joseph showed for his father when he died! For whom do you feel the same sentiment? Praise God for blessing you with the presence of these people. Pray also for those around you who are mourning. Pray for opportunities to compassionately serve them.

Joseph made a promise that he would bury his father in Canaan. So Joseph asked for Pharaoh's permission to fulfill that promise, a request that Pharaoh granted (vv. 5–6). Have you made any promises lately? Pray for the strength to stay true to your word (Matt 5:37).

Goshen. ⁹Chariots and horsemen also went up with him, so it was a very large entourage.

¹⁰When they came to the threshing floor of Atad on the other side of the Jordan, they mourned there with very great and bitter sorrow. There Joseph observed a seven-day period of mourning for his father. ¹¹When the Canaanites who lived in the land saw them mourning at the threshing floor of Atad, they said, "This is a very sad occasion for the Egyptians." That is why its name was called Abel Mizraim, which is beyond the Jordan.

¹²So the sons of Jacob did for him just as he had instructed them. ¹³His sons carried him to the land of Canaan and buried him in the cave of the field of Machpelah, near Mamre. This is the field Abraham purchased as a burial plot from Ephron the Hittite. ¹⁴After he buried his father, Joseph returned to Egypt, along with his brothers and all who had accompanied him to bury his father.

¹⁵When Joseph's brothers saw that their father was dead, they said, "What if Joseph bears a grudge and wants to repay us in full for all the harm we did to him?" ¹⁶So they sent word to Joseph, saying, "Your father gave these instructions before he died: ¹⁷'Tell Joseph this: Please forgive the sin of your brothers and the wrong they did when they treated you so badly.' Now please forgive the sin of the servants of the God of your father." When this message was reported to him, Joseph wept. ¹⁸Then his brothers also came and threw themselves down before him; they said, "Here we are; we are your slaves." ¹⁹But Joseph answered them, "Don't be afraid. Am I in the place of God? ²⁰As for you, you meant to harm me, but God intended it for a good purpose, so he could preserve the lives of many people, as you can see this day. ²¹So now, don't be afraid. I will provide for you and your little children." Then he consoled them and spoke kindly to them.

²²Joseph lived in Egypt, along with his father's family. Joseph lived 110 years. ²³Joseph saw the descendants of Ephraim to the third generation. He also saw the children of Makir the son of Manasseh; they were given special inheritance rights by Joseph.

CONTEMPLATE

Genesis 50:15–21

READ. Read the passage twice. Choose a verse to dwell on that speaks to you. Repeat it until it begins to take root. Consider verse 20 or 21.

MEDITATE. How did Joseph demonstrate both wisdom and compassion? Have you seen God bring good through something evil or trying in your life?

PRAY. Ask God to make you an ambassador of wisdom, mercy, peace, and provision for others. If you have not yet seen good come from a past evil in your life, ask for eyes to see and ears to hear Him at work. Praise Him that His compassions never fail (Lam 3:22).

CONTEMPLATE. Take a few moments to sit with Him. Rest in confidence that He takes any negative situation and then works for the good of those who love Him, who have been called according to His purpose (Rom 8:28).

²⁴Then Joseph said to his brothers, "I am about to die. But God will surely come to you and lead you up from this land to the land he swore on oath to give to Abraham, Isaac, and Jacob." ²⁵Joseph made the sons of Israel swear an oath. He said, "God will surely come to you. Then you must carry my bones up from this place." ²⁶So Joseph died at the age of 110. After they embalmed him, his body was placed in a coffin in Egypt.

JOURNAL

Genesis 50:22–26

REFLECT AND WRITE.

- How were Joseph's words in verse 24 prophetic?

- How was Joseph's burial different from Jacob's (see Gen 49:29—50:14)? Why would Joseph not have been buried with his ancestors?

- In what ways did Joseph exemplify godly character? How did Joseph serve as a type of redeemer? Reflect on areas in your life where you can become more like Joseph.

RESOURCES

Additional articles, developed by *The Abide Bible* team, are available for free on the Thomas Nelson Bibles website to supplement your Scripture engagement endeavor, to let "the word of Christ dwell in you richly" (Col 3:16).

HOW TO ABIDE IN GOD'S WORD: Learn how to come to the Scriptures in a manner that promotes a thriving, living, transforming relationship with Christ.

5 STEPS TO ENGAGE WITH THE BIBLE: Following these five steps will help you prepare to engage with God's Word so it becomes more personally meaningful and transformative in your life.

CHRIST, THE CENTER OF SCRIPTURE: It is through the Bible that we meet and know Christ. When we grow in our love for Christ, we grow in our love of Scriptures.

HOW IS SCRIPTURE ENGAGEMENT DIFFERENT FROM BIBLE STUDY? Scripture engagement is a complement to deep study of the Scriptures, engaging both the mind and the heart for a deepened relationship with God and a changed life.

SCRIPTURE ENGAGEMENT AND THE SPIRITUAL DISCIPLINES: Spiritual disciplines are means to saturate our lives with the Bible, engaging with it so that our lives are transformed.

HOW NOT TO READ THE BIBLE: God's Word is good and profitable, but there are some ways of approaching the Bible that can end up restricting spiritual growth.

Find these articles and more *Abide Bible Journal* resources
thomasnelsonbibles.com/abide-bible-journals